LAS VEGAS & VICINITY DAYTRIPPIN'

A GUIDE TO ADVENTURES BOTH IN, AND WITHIN TRAVELING DISTANCE OF LAS VEGAS, NEVADA

(TRIPS, NOT CHIPS)

By Russell & Kathlynn Spencer

Gem Guides Book Co.

Baldwin Park, CA

ISBN# 978-0-9664055-2-1
First Printing 2007

Other "Windshield Adventuring" books by the authors:

Mojave Desert Windshield Adventures
ISBN# 0-9664055-8-7
California's Highway 395 Windshield Adventures
ISBN#0-9664055-9-5
Santa Monica to Monterey, California's SR-1 Windshield Adventures
ISBN#0-9664055-3-6
Windshield Adventuring Through the Mojave Desert
ISBN#0-9664055-1-X (No longer in print)
Windshield Adventuring in Southern & Central Nevada
ISBN#0-9664055-4-4 (No longer in print)

Published and Distributed by

Gem Guides Book Co.

315 Cloverleaf Drive, Suite F
Baldwin Park, CA 91706
626-855-1611

Printed in the United States of America

EXPLORING LAS VEGAS AND THE SURROUNDING AREAS
INTRODUCTION

This book contains numerous trips which can be made from Las Vegas within a day.

Much of the time spent preparing this book was doing research in addition to visiting the actual attractions. In addition to our research and physical inspection, we send out "fact check" letters to the various attractions in order to assure the information we are including in all of our publications in accurate and current. NOTE: Our website at: www.windshieldadventures.com, has an updates section for current information on attractions included in our publications. (The title page of this book contains a list of our other books which are currently available.) .

SECTION "A" (IN & SOUTH OF LAS VEGAS)

(Initially it was our intention to include the hotel/casinos in the Las Vegas area. Upon checking on the number of the existing hotel/casinos in the Las Vegas area and finding the number in excess of 500, we have elected not to itemize them in this publication. The Las Vegas Visitor Bureau, or "Las Vegas Hotel/Casinos" on the internet can provide current and accurate listings.)
Attractions in and around Las Vegas
Attractions to the south of Las Vegas (A trip along I-15 from the California border to Las Vegas)

SECTION "B" (EAST OF LAS VEGAS)

Boulder City & Hoover Dam
A loop trip from Boulder City along Lake Mead to the Valley of Fire, Moapa Valley & return to Las Vegas (Side Trip#1: Arizona Hwy 93 south to Willow Beach, Chloride, Kingman and Route 66 to Oatman. Side Trip #2: Highway 95 south to I-40 with side trips to Techatticup in El Dorado Canyon, Cottonwood Cove on Lake Mojave, Christmas Tree Pass, side trip to Laughlin Nevada and Oatman Arizona & Fort Piute site/ruins.)

SECTION "C" (WEST OF LAS VEGAS)

Red Rock Canyon Loop Trip: Includes Red Rock Canyon State Park, Spring Mountain Ranch State Park and Bonnie Springs Ranch/Old Nevada
I-15 in Baker to the I-15 in Las Vegas, "The scenic route" Includes: Pahrump, Tecopa Hot Springs, China Ranch Date Farm/Oasis & Castles in Clay.
Death Valley National Park: Includes attractions found within the park and in Panamint Valley to the west of the park plus alternate routes into Southern California.

SECTION "D" (NORTH OF LAS VEGAS)

Highway 95 from Las Vegas 208 miles to Tonopah Nevada. Includes; Mount Charleston area, Goldfield and access to other attractions. Side trips include: **Death Valley access #1** via Highway 373 which includes; Ash Meadows National Wildlife Refuge, Death Valley Junction/Amargosa Opera House to Furnace Creek. **Death Valley access #2** via Highway 374 which includes Rhyolite, and Titus Canyon to Stovepipe Wells. **Death Valley access #3** via Highway 267 to Scotty's Castle.

SECTION "E" ATTRACTIONS IN SOUTHERN UTAH

Highway I-15 from Mesquite to southwestern Utah. Includes: Virgin River Gorge Recreation Area, St George, Cedar City, Zion National Park & Mountain Meadows Monument.

LAS VEGAS, & VICINITY, DAYTRIPIN'
Acknowledgments

As we traveled the routes in this book and performed the research both before and after writing it, we had the pleasure of meeting many interesting and delightful people. We had also met many people when we did the prior books that this is perhaps one of the reasons that we wrote this, our latest "Windshield Adventuring" book.

We want to give a special thanks to all of the untold staff, including rangers and docents, at all of the museums, visitor centers, parks and other attractions, which we visited. These were the people who took the time and patience to answer our seemingly endless questions and who provided us the necessary information, which allowed us to complete an authentic and current travel book. We received so much help from so many people that it was really gratifying.

An extra special thanks goes to all of those who took the time to review the "fact check" letters, containing information pertinent to their particular attraction, returning the edited information to us, which has enabled us to present as accurate a book as possible to our readers.

Use of the graphic materials contained in this book, which was obtained from: The State of Nevada Department of Transportation, The Nevada Division of State Parks, The Bureau of Land Management, The National Park Service, Western National Parks Association, The U. S. Fish & Wildlife Service, The Nuclear Security Administration, Nevada State Museum and Historical Society, Las Vegas Natural History Museum, Clark County Heritage Museum, Boulder City/Hoover Dam Historical Association, Federal Bureau of Reclamation, Forever Resorts/Black Canyon Adventures, Lake Mead Recreation Area, Lake Mead Cruises, Gold road Mine Tours, China Ranch & the Goldfield Chamber of Commerce and all other sources as stated within the publication, implies no copyright of that material by the authors. The use of pictures obtained from- implies no copyright of that material by the authors.

All other materials in this book, including photographs & text, are the property of the authors.

COVER PICTURES (From top center clockwise) #1 **Topoc Gorge**, Page 48 **Mine Tours**; 3 individual mine tours; Pages 38, 42 & 88. **Attractions in Las Vegas, Nevada, downtown and the "strip,"** Pages 4 – 18. **Hoover Dam & Lake Mead Recreation area**; Pages 24, 26 – 32 & 35 & 44 & 46. **Death Valley National Park**, Page 68. **Zion National Park**, Page 96. **London Bridge, Lake Havasu**, Page 48. **THE Las Vegas Sign**, Page 20. **Red Mountain Areas; Red Rock Canyon**; Page 57 & **Valley of Fire**, Page 31. **Rhyolite** ghost town, Page 93. Center Picture; **Ballarat area,** Page 77.

No promotional consideration was requested, nor obtained, during the production of this work.

TABLE OF CONTENTS
SECTION "A" LAS VEGAS & SOUTH ALONG THE I-15

SECTION B EAST OF LAS VEGAS
TRIP #B-1 LAS VEGAS TO BOULDER CITY & HOOVER DAM

TRIP B-2 WEST SHORE OF LAKE MEAD/VALLEY OF FIRE/MOAPA VALLEY/LAS VEGAS

TRIP #B-3, A TRIP FROM HOOVER DAM DOWN ARIZONA HIGHWAY 93

DANGERS IN AND AROUND ABANDONED MINES
(We have reprinted this notice, not because one might fall into a mine
shaft on the Las Vegas Strip, but when traveling in more primitive areas
it is a good idea to be mindful of the possible dangers.)

Almost the entire Nevada landscape, along with much of this area of California and Arizona, is covered with mines, many abandoned and some still being worked.

The information contained herein was obtained from the Bureau of Abandoned Mine Lands, Nevada Division of Minerals

SHAFTS: The collar or top of a mineshaft is especially dangerous. One can simulate the fall down a deep shaft by jumping off of a tall building. It is quite easy to slide down into the awaiting shaft as the result of decomposing rock or rotten timbers.

WATER: Standing water can conceal holes in the floor that could be deep enough to drown you. It is usually impossible to estimate the depth of water.

LADDERS: Common sense should tell us about the possibility of rotten or broken rungs, often the result of dry rot.

CAVE-INS: Just walking or talking within a mineshaft can create enough vibration to cause a cave-in. Even if the cave-in doesn't kill the explorer, starvation, gradual suffocation, or dying of thirst can be the result of a cave-in.

BAD TIMBERS: That strong looking timber at the opening of the shaft can in fact be so rotten that it is barely holding up its own weight. What could be just a "touch" to that timber could result in a "cave in."

BAD AIR: Poisonous gasses can often accumulate in low areas or along the floor of a mine. When walking into the mine and breathing good air it is possible to stir up the gasses from along the floor which are waiting to be inhaled on the way back out of the mine.

RATTLESNAKES: What better place for these poisonous reptiles to hide from the summer head and search for rodents than inside the mouth of a tunnel?

EXPLOSIVES: Many abandoned mines contain old explosives that were generally left behind because they were too dangerous to move. Sometimes it only takes a touch to explode old dynamite.

BOOBY TRAPS & ILLEGAL ACTIVITIES: There have been many cases where mines have been booby trapped either by someone who was secretly working the mine, or by someone using the mine for illegal purposes such as a methamphetamine lab.

IN THE EVENT OF A MINE ACCIDENT: No inexperienced person should attempt to rescue the victim of a mining accident. Notify the local sheriff in the event of a mine accident.

SECTION "A" LAS VEGAS & SOUTH
SECTION A

FEATURES AND ATTRACTIONS

A BRIEF HISTORY OF THE LAS VEGAS AREA

The recorded history of Southern Nevada begins in February of 1776 when Frey Francisco Garces crossed over near what is now Laughlin. This trip was an attempt to open a land route between Tucson, Arizona and California. This Franciscan was a lone white man whom the friendly Mojave led to the coast of California. On March 4, 1776 the small party crossed the Colorado River. He was the first non-native American to enter the area that we now know as Nevada.

It was January of 1830 when Rafael Rivera became the first non-native American to enter the Las Vegas Valley. Rivera was scouting a trail for a sixty-man trading party from New Mexico. As a result of the water and greenery here the area was named Las Vegas (Spanish for "The Meadows.") The springs located at what is now Las Vegas became a vital part of the Old Spanish Trail that today closely follows I-15 through Nevada. It soon became the trade route between the Mexican settlements at opposite the trail.

The Old Spanish Trail covered a total of 1,120 miles as it wound its way from Santa Fe around the Grand Canyon and several natural barriers on its way to Southern California. Some 130 miles of the trail cross what is now Clark County, Nevada. The 55 miles of road between Muddy River in the east and Las Vegas was called "Journada del Muerto," (The Journey of Death) as this was the longest stretch of the entire trail without water.

In 1844 John C. Fremont's mapping of the route which opened the trail for extensive travel. It became known by many as the "longest, crookedest, most arduous pack mule route in the history of America."

Not only was the trail itself a test, there were numerous Indian problems along the route. The Paiutes took not only goods but also travelers who were used and sold as slaves.

Once this route was opened trains of as many as a hundred traders would head west along the route with textiles, woven and manufactured goods to trade for horses and mules. These traders would often return with as many as a thousand head of cattle, many of which it is suspected were stolen from the missions and from the ranchos of California.

The Old Spanish Trail was in use primarily from 1830 to 1848 when the sovereignty of the area passed to the United States of America.

Between 1860 and 1924 a more southerly route to Southern California was developed as an alternate route to the Mormon settlement in San Bernardino. This trail, the Arrowhead Trail, swung south through the Henderson and Searchlight area and on through Nipton.

This road was a popular automobile route from 1914 to 1924 as it was claimed to be an "all-weather" route.

In 1850 the United States Congress established the Utah Territory. This new territory comprised most of what are now Utah, Nevada and Idaho and was placed under the control of Brigham Young who was the Territorial Governor and leader of the Mormon Church in Salt Lake City.

Young, who was the colonizer, immediately dispatched parties through the territory. Some 6 miles south of Carson City, at a spot called Genoa, the first permanent settlement in Nevada was established. Many of the areas within the state had ample water and rich enough soil to allow farming and ranching. The majority of the earliest settlement of Nevada came from the expansion of the Mormon population from Utah. This expansion went as far west as San Bernardino, California. While initially the westward movement of the Mormons was the result of natural expansion, some of the early settlements in Nevada were in part developed because of the possibility of conflict between the Mormons and United States Government troops.

In 1855 Mormons established a fort surrounding 8 houses at "The Meadows," Las Vegas. The purpose was primarily to protect the travelers along the Old Spanish Trail, to convert the Paiute Indians while at the same time cultivate the land to provide food for the travelers. The ranch was headquartered at what is now North Las Vegas Boulevard and Washington Street. The remaining structure, one of the houses, is the oldest building in Nevada.

During the mid-1850s the relationship between the Mormon population in Utah and the United States Government deteriorated. By 1857 the relationship had soured to the point where the U. S. Mail was stopped at the border and U. S. Army troops were moving towards the Utah border. Mormon "pioneer" settlement groups were sent into Nevada to search out new settlement locations to be used in the event that hostilities did break out. Panaca, located in Lincoln County was one of these settlements.

In 1857 Young recalled most of his settlers to Salt Lake City. In 1858 the Mormons left the "fort" in Las Vegas. Using the abandoned fort as headquarters, the surrounding 800 acres were farmed by several different parties. The entire area became a large cattle ranch from 1866 to 1904.

On March 2, 1861 by an act signed by Congress the area achieved territorial status thus separating it from Utah. Statehood for Nevada came on October 31, 1864 as the 36th state. Some 11,000 square miles around Las Vegas had remained as a part of the state of Arizona at the time Nevada became a state. It wasn't until 2 years later that the current state boundaries were achieved by an act of Congress.

A survey done in 1870 placed much of what had been western Utah into eastern Nevada. This survey had far reaching effects upon eastern Clark and Lincoln Counties. The taxes in non-Mormon Nevada were much higher that in Utah. As a result of the change of states by survey most of the Mormon settlers in what was now eastern Nevada packed up and moved back into Utah.

In the Moapa valley area these departing settlers left miles of irrigation canals, cleared and irrigated fields and many years of labor behind as they moved across the border.

In 1875 Conrad Kiel and his brother established Kyle (Kiel) Ranch is the intersection of Carey and Losee Road in North Las Vegas. This became only the second major ranch in the valley during the 19th century. There was much violence at this ranch and in 1884 both Kiels, Edwin and William, were found murdered.

Of these two historic sites, only the old Mormon Fort site (now the Old Las Vegas Mormon State Historic Park) is open to the public. (Page 6) The Kyle (Kiel) Ranch is currently under restoration and not open to the public. (Page 7)

In 1903 the San Pedro, Los Angeles and Salt Lake Railroad purchased both ranches. In 1905 as the result of the auctioning of 1,200 lots in a single day by the railroad, the city of Las Vegas was formed.

Las Vegas began life as a tent town as workers came into the area to work on the railroad. These temporary structures gradually gave way to more permanent structures as a city gave birth to itself.

The final spike marking the completion of the railroad from Salt Lake City to Los Angeles, California was driven on January 30, 1905, 4.6 miles northeast of Jean Nevada at a spot marked on the frontage road paralleling I-15.

The railroad and Las Vegas' water supply were the reasons that Las Vegas stayed alive for the next 20 years.

In 1910 Nevada became the last western state to pass laws eliminating casino type gambling. The new Nevada gambling law was so restraining it even prohibited flipping a coin to see who would buy the drinks! This opened the door for "password" gambling. If you knew the password, you could come in and gamble.

1911 saw the incorporation of Las Vegas as a city by the Nevada State Legislature.

In 1931 Las Vegas appeared immune to the financial effects of the Depression. The railroad was still a major source of employment in the valley, but gambling had just that year been made legal again in Nevada. Work was starting by over 5,000 workers on Boulder Dam just some 30 miles away in Black Canyon.

The Las Vegas area seemed to grow for many reasons with Clark County reaching a population of 16,000+ by 1940.

In 1941 the first hotel/casino on the "Strip", the El Rancho Vegas, opened.

World War II saw the U. S. Army Air Force come to the Las Vegas area and open an aircraft machine gun school.

In 1946 Bugsy Siegal opened the Flamingo Hotel at about the same time that the State of Nevada levied their first gaming taxes. This began an era in which it is reported that the mobsters of the east coast began to parlay millions into building a series of hotel casinos, not only along the strip but also in the downtown Las Vegas area.

In 1966 the purchase of the Desert Inn by millionaire Howard Hughes started a trend which would result in sweeping changes to Las Vegas. Corporate America was now becoming involved in the gambling/hotel business.

Today, the city of Las Vegas has become a family travel destination with the revenue from the majority of the casino/hotels being designed to satisfy stock holders and the mob presence appears to have disappeared, almost! One major exception is that the mayor of Las Vegas at this writing was the one-time lawyer for the mob bosses who had run numerous casinos in Las Vegas.

ATTRACTIONS IN THE LAS VEGAS AREA

Just a brief note regarding the attractions found in the Las Vegas Area: Over the last 40+ years your author has watched numerous attractions, including museums, located inside or in conjunction with casinos, folds their tents and move away. While we have included some features and attractions found within casinos, we have endeavored to include only those which appear to be permanent in nature and appealed to the most people.

And yes, there are numerous galleries and artifact exhibits to be found in the hotel/casinos in Las Vegas. Many of these exhibits are permanent and other come through the area on tour. We have found it best to check which of these exhibits/exhibitions are available at the time we are in Las Vegas.

THE MILITARY'S PRESENCE IN THE LAS VEGAS AREA

NELLIS AIR FORCE BASE
(702) 652-1110
www.nellisafb

Since the inception of Nellis Army Air Force Base in the 1940's and the Nuclear Test Range, opened in the 1950's, the military has played an important role in the growth of both southern and central Nevada.

Approximately one fourth of the Air Force Base includes the Desert National Wildlife Refuge. The refuge was formed in 1936 to protect the Desert Bighorn Sheep. Today the total size of the range is about 3 million acres and is the largest military land-based military range in the United States.

In June of 1941 construction began on a gunnery school at Nellis Air Force Base. During the next 4 1/2 years some 50,000 men were trained as machine gunners for B-17 and B-29 bombers. The payroll from this facility has always had an effect on the areas surrounding the facility. The high-performance United States Air Force flight team, the Thunderbirds, is based at Nellis Air Force Base. NOTE: Since 9-11, Nellis Air Force Base, including the museum, is not open to the public.

There are various facilities located in different areas of this massive facility. The majority of the "standard" Air Force facilities are located northeast of downtown Las Vegas with the runways visible from Las Vegas Motor Speedway, located across the street in addition to many of the downtown Las Vegas hotel rooms. Further to the north is found the Air Force Test Center which is located east of Tonopah, Nevada and was once the home of the F-117 Stealth Fighter. Toward the east is found the Groom Dry Lake Area (Area 51) which doesn't exist according to the armed guards who monitor the area.

THE NEVADA TEST SITE
(702) 295-0944
www.nv.doe.gov

Photo courtesy of National Nuclear Security Administration,
Nevada Site Office

In addition to the Nellis test range this area also contains the 1,375 square mile Nevada Test Site (NTS). This was the nuclear test range opened in the 1950's and saw some 928 nuclear tests until 1992 when the current test ban went into effect. The tests were moved from the Pacific Islands to this location during the 1950's because of the expense and logistic problems encountered in the mid-pacific test areas. Of the nuclear tests performed here, 100 were above ground and there were occasions when the citizens of Las Vegas could see the blast from town. The total size of the combined facilities is 5,470 square miles!

Scheduled tours of the Nevada Test Site are open to the public. There are numerous restrictions on these tours and prior arraignments must be made. For information on tours contact:

U. S. Department of Energy, National Nuclear Security Administration,
Nevada Site Office,
Visit Coordination Staff,
P.O, Box 98518,
Las Vegas, Nv.89193-8518
(702) 295-0944,
www.nv.doe.gov/nts/tours.htm

ATOMIC TESTING MUSEUM (Fee)
755 East Flamingo Road, (702) 794-5151 www.nv.doe.gov/nts/museum.htm
Mon-Sat. 9am – 5pm, Sunday 1 pm – 5pm

An affiliate of the Smithsonian Institution, the museum officially opened in February of 2005. The museum contains over 8,000 square feet of information on the history of the Nevada Test Site. Some of the exhibits seen here have been under development since 1997. The visitor will see permanent exhibits, first person narratives, large artifacts, environmental re-creations, and stunning graphics, many of which have never before been seen by the public.

The map below shows attractions in the north section of Las Vegas

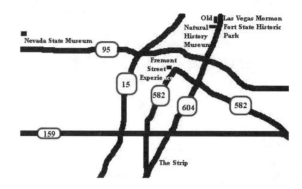

OLD LAS VEGAS MORMON STATE HISTORICAL PARK
500 E. Washington Ave.
Las Vegas, NV. 89101
(Behind the Las Vegas Natural History Museum 3 blocks north of Highways 93 & 95)
(702) 486-3511, www.park.nv.gov, email address; cmack@parks.nv.gov
Entrance fee
The park is open all year (except Sundays) from 8:00 am to 4:30 pm. Historic Site & Gift Shop

THE MORMON FORT AS IT APPEARED IN 1929
Photo courtesy of Nevada State Parks

Water and meadows along the hottest and driest section of the Old Spanish Trail made this a natural stopping place.

On June 14, 1855, Mormons from Salt Lake City arrived and began the construction of a fort. The fort was 150 feet square with 14' high walls. Land was cleared for crops and an irrigation system was built.

In 1857, 3 months before the general recall of the Mormons to Utah, the fort was closed and the Mormon settlers returned to Salt Lake City.

In the mid 1860s Octavious Decatur Gass acquired the site and began using the site as a ranch, blacksmith shop and a supply center for travelers along the road from Salt Lake City to Southern California.

In 1881 Gass lost the ranch to foreclosure and Archibald Stewart and his wife Helen took over the ranch. Archibald was killed at the Kiel Ranch in 1884. The widow, Helen Stewart, continued to operate the ranch/supply center.

1902 saw the property, along with most of the land in the area, being sold to the San Pedro, Los Angeles and Salt Lake Railroad.

Beginning in 1905 the property was leased to various people and it became known as The Old Ranch.

In 1929 the Bureau of Reclamation leased the property and used it as a testing lab for materials to be used in the construction of Boulder Dam.

In 1991 ownership of the property was transferred to the Nevada State Park System who is currently in the process of restoring this historic landmark to its original condition.

KYLE RANCH (SITE)
100 Block of Carey, between Commerce & Losse
(North side of street, adjacent to Commercial Center)

At this point in time all that is located at this site is an old adobe shed, a shed which it is thought was built around 1856 which is located behind a wire fence.

This site is mentioned at this time because of its historic importance and plans for refurbishment the site by the city of North Las Vegas.

In 1992 the city of North Las Vegas had made plans and was preparing to begin the refurbishing of not only the site but also of the original ranch house which stood on the site. Just prior to the time that work was to begin on the project, the house burnt to the ground!

The vacant lot west of the fenced ranch site is slated to be a parking lot for the site and some grading has been started there.

In talking with the City of North Las Vegas we learned that completion of the existing adobe and installation of the parking lot while scheduled for January of 1999 and completion of the ranch house replica and completion of the park was projected for the year 2000 as of Spring of 2006 the work has not been done. The city has gone to the State of Nevada for funding and is also looking for donations to help complete the project.

FLOYD LAMB STATE PARK (To be returned to Las Vegas July 1, 2007 as a park)
9200 Tule Springs Road
Las Vegas, NV. 89131
(Located off of Highway 95, 15 miles north of downtown Las Vegas east off of Durango Road)
(702)486-5413 - Fee area.

Tule Springs dig site, assigned to the park was once the home of massive mammoths. Evidence suggests the presence of man here before 11,000 BC and perhaps hunting in the valley some 13,000 years ago. Tule Springs dig site is known as one of the best paleontology sites in the western United States.

In 1916 John Nay filed the first non-native American water rights claim in the area. Subsequently he began to cultivate the land and built the adobe hut (1914-1918) which stands here today.

In 1928 he sold the property however it remained vacant until 1941 when a Prosper Jacob Goumond acquired it. Goumond began creating a working ranch at the site. At about the same time Nevada changed its divorce laws making them the most flexible in the country. If you became a resident of Nevada for 6 weeks, you could claim residency and obtain a divorce at that time.

Goumond began to convert a part of his working ranch into a combination guest ranch that could accommodate 10 to 12 people who were living in Nevada awaiting their divorce.

The Tule Lake Springs Ranch offered all of the normal ranch activities plus a swimming pool, tennis courts, a shooting range (which is still there), dances and the proximity of the Las Vegas night life. The ranch was still a working ranch raising alfalfa, cattle and other live stock and garden vegetables for kitchen use. The ranch soon grew to 880 acres.

In 1964 Goumond died. His granddaughter sold the property to businessmen in 1959 and the site was purchased in 1964 by the city of Las Vegas for use as a city park.

In 1977 the state of Nevada acquired the property from the city of Las Vegas and named it Floyd Lamb Park after a state senator who had been instrumental in its acquisition.

The park has increased in size to just over 2,000 acres. The park is open for day use only and features numerous picnic sites around the lakes, many of which are covered. The lakes lay between the towering trees and rolling grassy hills. The 4 reed lined ponds are stocked with catfish in the summer and trout in the winter. A fishing license is required.

Directions to the park from Las Vegas via Highway 95 are found on page 79.

Photo courtesy of Nevada State Parks

8

NEVADA STATE MUSEUM and HISTORICAL SOCIETY
700 Twin Lakes Drive
Las Vegas, NV 89107
(Located in Lorenzi City Park: US 95 to Valley View Exit,
right on Bonanza, left on Twin Lakes Dr. – right into first park entrance)
(702) 486-5205. Fee

This state museum is located in a beautiful setting. Located in Las Vegas City Park it is situated on a lake and is surrounded by trees and rolling lawns.

Inside the museum, displays focus mostly on southern Nevada. Artifacts, books, maps, newspaper indexes photographs and manuscripts, relating to Nevada and Las Vegas history are available for research.

Photo Courtesy Nevada State Museum and Historical Society

The 35,000 square foot museum also contains specimens of Nevada's mammals and a collection of paleontological materials, minerals and Native American artifacts.

Displays and exhibits trace the history of the area from prehistoric man through the 20th century featuring a special display on the growth of the Las Vegas Valley during World War II and the beginning of the gambling and tourist attractions of today.

The museum store offers a wide variety of publications on Nevada and the Southwest in addition to Native American arts and crafts and is open the same hours as the museum. The museum is open daily from 9:00 to 5:00, it is closed on Thanksgiving, Christmas and New Years.

BIG SPRINGS
Almost directly across the freeway from the Nevada State Museum is the site of Big Springs. Big Springs, is in fact the birthplace of Las Vegas. At present there is no park or plaque, nothing to really mark the site.

It was at Big Springs that Antonio Armijo stopped in 1829-30 while traveling the route that was to become known as the Old Spanish Trail. It was at this site that John C. Fremont camped on May 3, 1844

LAS VEGAS NATURAL HISTORY MUSEUM
(Adjacent to The Mormon Fort Site, 3 blocks north of the junction of Highways 93 & 95))
900 Las Vegas Blvd. North
Las Vegas, NV 89101
(702) 384-3466
Open Daily 9 AM to 4 PM, Fee, Gift Shop

PHOTO COURTESY OF LAS VEGAS NATURAL HISTORY MUSEUM

The museum that brings "science to life" is the slogan of this 35,000 square foot museum. Animated exhibits, live animals, and rare animal mounts comprise the displays to bring natural history alive.

Virtually everyone enjoys watching the five robotic dinosaurs go through their antics.There are dozens of species of mounted animals representing wildlife from all over the world.

In the marine room is a 3,000-gallon tank occupied by several varieties of sharks.

A great deal of the museum is dedicated to the younger set and features two rooms: The Young Scientist Center and The Education Center geared for learning by seeing and by doing. The museum is constantly updating and changing its exhibits.

The Wild Nevada Room features the harsh beauty of the desert. Its unique plants and animals from the majestic bighorn sheep and the desert tortoise to the rattlesnake, can all be found within 100 miles of Las Vegas. Visitors experience Nevada through sight, touch, sounds and scents. The large glass case allows the visitor to visually follow burrowing rodents under the desert floor where they escape the heat of summer.

The African Savanna gallery presents the beauty of the Serengeti, highlighting a watering hole scene. The African Rainforest features the diverse life found in the African Jungle. The Out of Africa exhibit also features recreations of three extinct primates dating back 3 ½ million years. Shark feeding time is 2 PM on Saturday.

The museum is open daily from 9 AM to 4 PM except Thanksgiving and Christmas. The museum features an extensive and creatively stocked gift shop.

CLARK COUNTY MUSEUM

(A part of the Cultural Division of the Clark County Parks & Recreation Department)
(East of Boulder Highway, South of Horizon Drive, Hwy. 95 access)
1830 South Boulder Highway
Henderson, NV. 89015
(702) 455-7955, www.co.clark.nv.us

This unique museum features many types of exhibits covering different periods of the past. There is even a look at the "newer west."

Inside the museum is found the story of Southern Nevada, from prehistoric times through the 20th century. Many of these exhibits are life-sized dioramas with movement activated narratives. Also located in the museum is a rather complete gift shop with a large selection of books and other publications covering points of interest and historical information on the area.

The museum grounds have a variety of interesting historical items. Right outside the door of the museum is a 1918 steam engine that is not far from the railroad caboose awaiting the visitor's inspection. The caboose is right of the railroad depot that served the ill-fated Las Vegas-Boulder City Railroad from 1931 to 1932, when the line shut down passenger service. The depot is open to visitors and stands equipped, as it probably was when it was in operation. The depot also features a sound activated narration.

Heritage Street features houses, which were relocated to this site and range in age from the pioneer era through the World War II era. The majority of the homes are open for inspection.

Behind the museum building, a walkway winds the visitor through a resurrected ghost town featuring; structures, mining equipment, vintage vehicles and an outdoor program area where special events and various programs are scheduled.

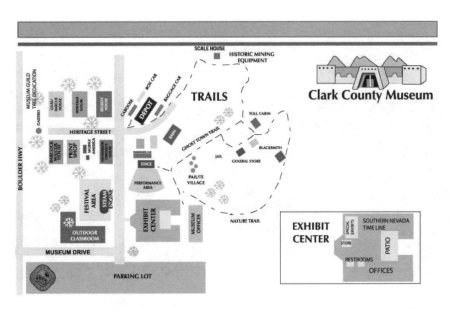

Map Courtesy of the Clark County Heritage Museum

OTHER ATTRACTIONS AND ACTIVITIES IN THE LAS VEGAS AREA

LAS VEGAS MOTOR SPEEDWAY
7000 Las Vegas Blvd. N
(800) 644-4444
www.lvms.com

Located some 12 miles north of downtown Las Vegas and across from the eastern end of the Nellis Air Force Base runway we found quite a unique adventure. The Las Vegas Motor Speedway which is located between I-15 and Las Vegas Boulevard (there's that famous road again) can provide more than spectator excitement for the visitor!

Since 1996 this complex has offered racing fans excitement from its internationally known 1.5 mile speedway, which features NASCAR racing. Additionally, this complex also features a ¼ mile drag strip, NHRA racing, along with a major dirt track, bull ring and go-cart tracks.

Visitors to the track will also experience a great number of numbers of aircraft taking off and landing at Nellis Air Force Base. The roar of the F-15s, F-10 Warthogs and other jets is almost constant at the track which is adjacent to the raceway.

In addition to a regular racing schedule, the facility also offers tours of the speedway facility, in addition to several driving schools and ride-along experiences open to the public.

One of the driving schools is the Richard Petty Driving Experience. Visitors have the opportunity to either ride-along with a professional driver in a NASCAR type vehicle on the 1 & ½ mile super speedway at speeds of 160 to 170 miles per hour, or after training, actually driving these cars at speeds in the range of 130 miles per hour.

Your author, after driving some "hot laps" at the Las Vegas Motor Speedway

FREMONT STREET EXPERIENCE
Fremont Street, Between Las Vegas Blvd. and Main Street (5 Blocks)
FREE

Opened in December of 1995 at a cost of some 70 million dollars, this unusual "experience" has entertained millions of people with hourly shows from dusk to midnight with a different performance every show.

The Fremont Experience features not only the largest LED display in the world, over 12 million lights, but also the sound is delivered through a 550,000 watt sound system. A recent 17 million dollar renovation has increased the visual display.

In addition to a variety of kiosks, many of which are open during the day, entertainment and special events take place at the experience in the evening.

Everything from wandering troubadours to bands to magical acts, caricature artists and magicians are to found along the five blocks which comprise the Fremont Experience. Bring the kids and remember that the show is free.

Information: www.vegasexperience.com

TOURS OF THE AREA SURROUNDING LAS VEGAS
(We recommend checking with the local chamber or visitor center for tour referrals)

One of the major purposes of this publication is to present attractions which are not only within the greater Las Vegas area but are located within a day's travel from Las Vegas.

Currently there are numerous commercial tours with a wide variety of places to choose from available from Las Vegas. There are one day bus trips to Zion and Bryce Canyon National Parks located to the north. Helicopters and fixed wing aircraft stand ready to take tourists on an excursion to Grand Canyon National Park and to other scenic spots throughout the southwest.

When in Las Vegas it is difficult not to notice the number of helicopters flying overhead, day or night. The majority of these are tourists getting a view of Las Vegas and some of the other nearby attractions.

There are even wedding tours available were a couple may be married at Grand Canyon or flying over Las Vegas in a helicopter (watch for falling rice!).

ATTRACTIONS ALONG THE LAS VEGAS STRIP

There are numerous attractions to be found in and around the hotel/casinos located along Las Vegas Boulevard, "The Strip." We will give a brief description of some of these attractions which appear to be permanent and appeal to the greatest number of people. These attractions will, with the exception of the monorail/trams, appear in alphabetic order.

The majority of the newer hotel casinos offer "themed" architectural designs in their basic motif. The majority of the larger hotels offer extensive shopping facilities.

In Las Vegas it is possible to have breakfast under the Eiffel Tower, lunch inside a pyramid and dinner followed by a gondola ride through a Venetian setting.

THE LAS VEGAS MONORAIL (MGM GRAND TO SAHARA) Fee
Monday – Thursday 7 am – 2 am and Friday - Sunday 7am – 3am
Traveling along the east side of "The Strip," the monorail stops at MGM Grand, Bally's/Paris, Flamingo, Harrah's/Imperial Palace, Las Vegas Convention Center, Las Vegas Hilton and the Sahara.

THE MANDALAY BAY – LUXOR – EXCALIBUR TRAM

STRIP HOTEL TRAMS Free
In addition to this monorail there are two trams which service specific hotels along the Strip: Mirage-Treasure Island Tram & Mandalay Bay-Luxor-Excalibur Tram

SOME OF THE MORE POPULAR/PERMANENT STRIP ATTRACTIONS

AUTO MUSEUM – IMPERIAL PALACE
9:30am – 9:30pm daily

Over 250 classic, antique and special interest automobiles are located on the 5th floor of the Imperial Palace's parking garage. In addition to viewing these beauties, it is possible to buy and sell them. Additional information: (702) 794-3174, www.imperialpalace.com/autos, e-mail: info@autocollections.com.

CIRCUS ACTS/AMUSEMENT PARK – CIRCUS CIRCUS HOTEL

From 11am to midnight, every ½ hour what are described as "world renowned circus acts" perform different live acts free at the carnival midway.

Located behind the Circus Circus Hotel the Adventure Dome Amusement Park offers 5 acres of rides and adventure attractions geared for all types of fun and thrill seekers, all for just one price. The park opens daily at 10am and for closing times you may call (702) 794-3939.

ANCIENT EGYPTION ATTRACTIONS – LUXOR HOTEL

From the pyramid shaped exterior with the sphinx at the entrance, to the extensive statuary and interior décor the Luxor Hotel does have the ability to take the visitor back to an ancient place and time.

Not only is the replica of the contents of King Tutankhamun's Tomb and the museum's treasures complete, but they are also meticulously placed as they were found by the Carter expedition. This exhibit is open from 9am to 11pm.

"In Search of the Obelisk" is an adventure ride/film which takes the audience through a series of chases and escapes.

This Anubis resides in the duplicate of King Tut's tomb at the Luxor

Also showing at the Luxor is the film "Mystery of the Nile" which takes the viewer on an adventure filled trip down the Nile River.

LION HABITAT – MGM GRAND
11 am – 11pm Daily/Free
Information: (702) 891-7777

There are live lions inside the MGM Grand! Daily, noted lion authority Keith Evans transports several groups of his lions to a special enclosure inside the MGM Grand. Included in the enclosure are waterfalls, a pond, and overhangs and it is complete with clear heavy-duty walls to allow visitors an unobstructed view of the lions and the handlers who work with them.

A special entrance with a clear plastic ceiling, allows visitors to look up directly at any cats who might be on the top of the clear roof!

ATTRACTIONS FOUND AT THE MIRAGE
WHITE TIGERS, DOLPHIN AND EXTERIOR ANIMAL HABITAT

Behind the main hotel desk is one of the most unique aquariums in the world. Fifty three feet long, eight feet high and containing 20,000 gallons of exotic, salt water animal life. This display can help make those check-in times much shorter.

WHITE TIGER HABITAT

Located at the southern most Las Vegas Boulevard entrance to the Mirage, this unique setting offers the white tigers in a natural appearing habitat. With the top of the habitat open to the air, swimming pools and natural appearing "caves," the tigers appear to be totally at ease. The floor to ceiling glass is even slanted to assist in the tigers feeling of being in a natural environment. The tigers are rotated through the display. There are gift shops in the area of this display. (Exiting through this door and going south will give you access to the Forum Shops at Caesar-see below)

HERE KITTY, KITTY, KITTY!

16

THE SECRET GARDEN OF SEIGRIED & ROY AND THE DOLPHIN HABITAT
Fee – Call (702) 792-7889 for current information

Four pools containing approximately 2 ½ million gallons of water comprise this complex. It is extensively for research and training of the Atlantic Bottlenose Dolphin. They can be observed in the water through windows located in the side of the tank. Guided tours are included in the entrance fee.

In addition to the dolphin habitat, some of the world's most interesting and rarest animals are on view in naturalized habitat exhibits. White lions, white tigers, and elephants are just part of the secret garden.

THE MIRAGE VOLCANO
Every hour, on the hour from 7 pm to midnight, this spectacular attraction sprays flame 100 feet into the air, transforming waterfalls into torrents of what appears to be molten lava. The show goes on nightly, except when weather interferes.

* * * * * *

SHARK REEF - MANDALAY BAY
10am – 11pm
Fee area. (702) 632-7580 for information.

This attraction contains more than sharks. Over 1,200 different species are found here, in and out of the water. There are numerous displays and exhibits containing all forms of marine life from all around the world

The main attraction here is the shark reef itself. The total displacement of the shark reef, which is 22 feet deep, is reported to be almost 2,000,000 gallons containing 2,000 animals from 100 different species. Standing in the shark reef, one is completely surrounded by water with different species swimming around you.

In addition to regular admission to this attraction, educational sessions, including guided tours and classroom studies, are offered twice daily during the week for an additional fee. (702) 932-4555 is the contact number for tour information.

THE FORUM SHOPS AND LIVING STATUES AT CAESARS
10 am – 11pm Sun thru Thurs. (Until midnight Fri. & Sat)
(702) 893-4800

One of the older of the casino/hotel shopping opportunities, The Forum Shops have recently expanded to 643,000 square feet and now contains more than 160 shops and 13 specialty food shops.

One of the major attractions here are the two living statues which perform every hour, on the hour, from 10 am to 11 pm. These two statues are responsible for a large number of visitors to the Forum Shops Daily. The 50,000 gallon aquarium which surrounds the Atlantis Fountain is a tremendous draw, especially during the twice a day feedings.

LIBERACE MUSEUM.
1775 E Tropicana (at Spencer St.)
Las Vegas, NV 89119-6529
(702) 798-5595
Open 10 am to 5pm daily, 12 – 4 Sundays – Closed Mondays & major holidays, Fee area
Museum, café & store. Hotel shuttle service available, call for information.

The Liberace Museum was recently voted one of the most popular attractions in Nevada. Founded by the late entertainer, this museum features many examples of Liberace's lavish tastes.

Divided into two areas, the first area of the museum is devoted to his pianos and cars, while the second features the jewelry and costume collections. Additionally, this area contains his awards and a re-creation of one of the stars bedrooms. The "Grand Gallery" features a showcase of changing exhibitions

STAR TREK EXPERIENCE HILTON HOTEL
3000 S. Paradise, Las Vegas 89109
(702) 697-8700, Reservations: (702) 697-8752
Sun – Thurs 11 am to 10 pm, Fri & Sat 11am – 11pm
Several rides (Borg 4 D) restaurant, bar, promenade with shops

It is stated that this is the most complete collection of Star Trek materials found anywhere. In addition to the displays there are two exciting rides which take the visitor on adventures in the world of Star Trek.

The diners in Quark's Restaurant and bar are often greeted by various characters from Star Trek.

ALONG I-15 SOUTH OF LAS VEGAS,

It is estimated that over 1 million travelers cross the desert from Primm (the California/Nevada state line) to Las Vegas, Nevada every year. Most of these travelers are so intent on their destination that they are totally unaware of the history of the area they are traveling through.

WHISKEY PETE'S, PRIMM (STATELINE) NEVADA
Gas, Food, Lodging, Nevada Visitor Information Center, Factory outlet shopping
Visitor Information Center is located on the east side of the highway in front of the outlet stores

What are now several huge hotel/casinos, gas stations and factory outlet stores, was once the location of a 2-pump gas station in the middle of nowhere. Yes, there really was a "Whiskey Pete." Back in the old days when a two lane road crossed the desert into Las Vegas the operator of the gas station, whose real name has disappeared into history, acquired the name Whisky Pete, because of whiskey still he had in a cave across the highway from the gas station.

The stories say that the travelers who stopped to get just water from Whisky Pete were told to go back down the road and get their water from the same place that they had bought their gas!

Whiskey Pete was a curious man and so, as the stories have it, at his request he is buried nearby and facing the highway, so that he can see who drives by,

JEAN, NEVADA
Gas, Food, Lodging, Casinos

At the community of Jean, Nevada, located some 13 miles north of the California border, the off ramp to State Highway 64 can bring the traveler in touch with some of the more recent history of this area.

The large fenced compound located above the casino center is a prison. Many of the limousines seen in and around Las Vegas were built here by the inmates.

East on Highway 64 will take the traveler to Goodsprings.

GOODSPRINGS
Food

Seven miles west of Jean on State Highway 161 is the town of Goodsprings. Goodsprings was named for a cattleman named Joseph Good. The developer of this mining-ranching community was actually A. G. Campbell.

It was around 1856 when the Mormon settlers in Las Vegas first began to mine the area. The first of these mines was at Potosi, located north of the present location of Goodsprings; this was probably the oldest lode mine in Nevada.

In 1905, as a result of the proximity of the Los Angeles-Salt Lake City Railroad, mining increased in this area. In 1911 the narrow-gauge Yellow Pine Railroad began service between Jean and Goodsprings which further decreased ore transportation costs and further increased mining operations in the area. In 1916 Goodsprings reached the peak of its operations and boasted a population of some 800 residents.

This mining district produced the greatest variety of minerals found in the entire state of Nevada. Lead, zinc, gold, silver, copper, molybdenum, vanadium, cobalt, platinum, palladium, nickel and even uranium were mined in the area to a total of approximately $25,000,000.00.

Today Goodsprings sits as a small and historic mining town at an altitude of some 3,700 feet, surrounded by Joshua trees. The pioneer tavern, while it might appear closed, could just be open. Most of the people who now reside both here and in Sandy Valley, located to the west, are either retired or commute to work in the Las Vegas area.

Continuing westward, the area around Goodsprings is honeycombed with the remnants of old mining activity.

This sign at the southern end of the "strip" (Las Vegas Boulevard) has welcomed thousand of visitors every year
(For years this sign sat out in the desert, far from town, now it is well "inside" Las Vegas due to growth)

STATE HIGHWAY # 604, LAS VEGAS BLVD. THE "STRIP"

Going EAST of Highway 161; the stop sign east of the parking lot for the casino in Jean, Nevada marks State Highway #604 which parallels the I-15 Interstate Highway all of the way into Las Vegas. This is the "old" highway into Las Vegas and when it gets a little closer to town, will become Las Vegas Boulevard, the world famous "Strip."

Traveling this "frontage road" highway offers a chance to drive through some of yesterday's memories and offers an opportunity to stop and study the old motels of yesterday or watch the off-road racers charge across the desert on the racetrack, which parallels the roadway. As the roadway drops into the valley, it becomes Las Vegas Boulevard, "The Strip."

Some 4 ½ miles east of Jean there is a sign on this road which notes the nearby spot where the last spike was driven marking the completion of the railroad line from Salt Lake City, Utah to Los Angeles, California. This final spike was driven on January 30, 1905. Thus, the railroad formed a link between the East Coast and Southern California. It was primarily the railroad, which allowed the town of Las Vegas to exist, and then to grow into what it is today.

Nearing days end, over the mountains just west of Las Vegas

END OF SECTION "A"

SECTION B EAST OF LAS VEGAS

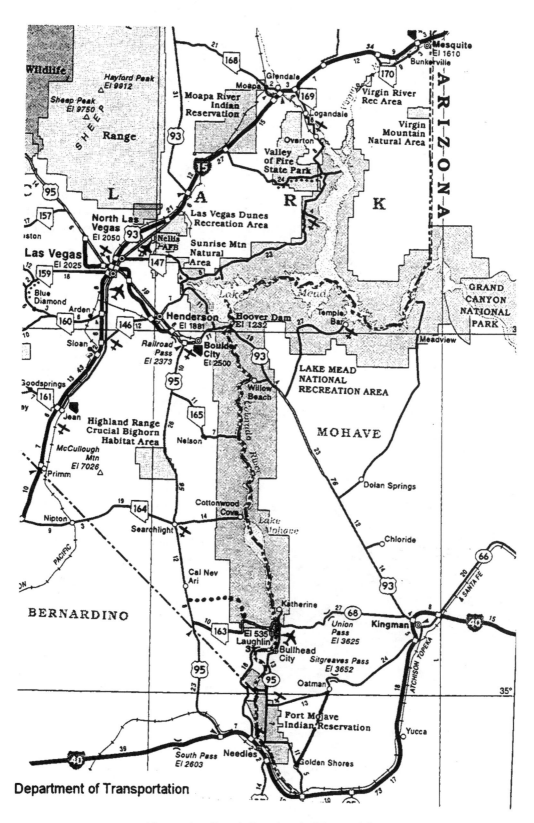

Map courtesy Nevada Department of Transportation

TRIP #B-1 LAS VEGAS TO HOOVER DAM VIA BOULDER CITY
LAS VEGAS TO HOOVER DAM
Highway 95 (515) South (Mile 0)

BOULDER JUNCTION
Mile 19
Take Highway 93 East
At this junction Highway 95 goes south to I-40
& covered in the trip to Laughlin

BOULDER CITY TURNOFF
Mile 22
Boulder City was born with the construction of Hoover Dam and built by the federal government. A location near the construction site was required for the 5,000 workers who arrived to build the massive dam. Today Boulder City is like a very quiet suburb of Las Vegas. Filled with lots of grass, shade trees and friendly people Boulder City does not fit in with the "Vegas" image. This is the only city in Nevada without gambling!

THE BOULDER CITY/HOOVER DAM MUSEUM
1305 Arizona Street
Boulder City, NV
(702) 294-1988
Open 10 - 5 Monday-Saturday & Sunday 12 - 5, Fee

The Boulder City/Hoover Dam Museum is located in the historic Boulder Dam Hotel. This museum offers the visitor a look at not only the history of this area but of Hoover Dam itself. The Boulder City Museum and Historical Association established the museum to commemorate and preserve the memory of the "31ers" as the dam builders were known. Between 90 and 120 men died during the construction of the dam.

The museum contains memorabilia, photos and an excellent movie that documents the extremes encountered in building the dam.

Hoover Dam under construction
Photo courtesy of the Boulder City/Hoover Dam Museum

By continuing east on Hotel Plaza you will return to Highway 93 just 7 miles from Hoover Dam.

HOOVER DAM /HOOVER DAM PARKING STRUCTURE
Mile 30
Museum, dam tours, gift shop, cafeteria
Information/tour reservations: (702) 494-2517, (800) 730-9097

Hoover Dam, Boulder Dam as it was called during its construction, was built at a cost of over $165 million dollars and was under construction from 1931 to 1935. The dam was constructed for several reasons, the primary reason being to control the flooding by the Colorado River. In addition to preventing flooding the dam also allows the stabilization of the water flow and provides electrical power for much of the southwestern portion of the country.

The dam is 726 feet high, 1,244 feet long, 45 feet wide at the top and 660 feet wide at the base. The dam contains some 3.25 million cubic yards of concrete.

The recently opened Visitor Center, located on the Nevada side of the dam, cost more to build and took longer to construct than the original dam itself!

The result is an interesting look at the dam through pictures, exhibits and tours. Yes, there are tours which can take the visitor deep into dam.

There is a safety inspection station one mile east of the dam on the Nevada side of the dam and nine miles east of the dam on the Arizona side. Due to security precautions as a result of 9-11 there ALL VEHICLES ARE SUBJECT TO INSPECTION, with virtually all RVs and other large vehicles normally being inspected. There can be extensive delays in crossing the dam as the result of these inspections.

On the north side of the dam, just up from the crosswalk leading to the Visitors Center, near the Nevada spillway is the Hoover Dam Snacketeria and Bookstore.

Photo courtesy of the Federal Bureau of Reclamation

HOOVER DAM HIGHWAY 93 BY-PASS. At this writing, a 2,000 foot long bridge, 1,500 feet south of Hoover Dam is under construction. The dam, which is scheduled for completion in 2008, will be 840 feet above the Colorado River. The bridge will be four lanes wide and will divert the heavy through Highway 93 traffic away from top of the dam. The current road along the top of the dam will remain open for use by Hoover Dam visitors.

BLACK CANYON/WILLOW BEACH RIVER ADVENTURES
Hacienda Hotel and Casino, Highway 93
(P.O. Box 60130) Boulder City, NV 89006
Transportation from major hotels in Las Vegas is available
Reservations & Information (800) 455-3490 www.blackcanyonriveradventures.com

Black Canyon River Adventures gives a whole new meaning to the phrase; "Cruising down the River!"

BLACK CANYON RIVER ADVENTURERS AT THE BASE OF HOOVER DAM
Photo courtesy of Forever Resorts/Black Canyon Adventures

There is no way of determining the exact number, perhaps hundreds of thousands, of visitors who have visited Hoover Dam since its opening in 1935/36. It is, however, safe to say that only a very few of them have seen the "monolith" from the river.

Looking up to the top of the dam, over 700 feet from the river, gives the traveler a whole new perspective. The dam itself is only a portion of the attractions found on this unusual adventure.

The dam was constructed in the narrows of Black Canyon, which is probably not what the riverboat skippers used to call this canyon. Black Canyon contained not only rapids and a strong current but also sandbars which also plagued their journey.

Today the heavy duty rafts of Black Canyon River Adventures glide through the canyon, heading south into area containing not only scenic geography and geology but, as the on-board guides point out, a landscape which contains big horn sheep, osprey and other birds and wildlife.

The tour includes lunch in a souvenir, insulated bag and a stop along the way to swim in the river, or just sit back and enjoy the scenery.

The raft portion of the tour terminates at Willow Beach Marina. Buses will take the adventurers from Willow Beach, back to the Hacienda Hotel office, or to their Las Vegas hotel.

TRIP B-2 (POSSIBLE LOOP TRIP)
WEST SHORE OF LAKE MEAD/VALLEY OF FIRE/MOAPA VALLEY/LAS VEGAS
Highway 95 (515), Highway 93, North Shore Scenic Drive (Hwy. 167), Hwy. 169 & I-15
(76 miles to junction Hwy 169 North & I-15. 46 miles to Las Vegas from169 North & I-15.

LAKE MEAD NATIONAL RECREATION AREA = FEE AREA
Park Phone # (702) 293-8997 Emergency # &02)293-8932

Mail; 601 Nevada Way, Boulder City, NV 89005 Website; www.nps.gov/lame

The Lake Mead National Recreational Area is comprised of 1,500,000 acres with six marinas on Lake Mead and three on Lake Mohave. Lake Mead has a shoreline of over 550 miles. In this vast recreational area there are numerous and varied attractions. It is advisable to check with the Alan Bible, or other visitor stations to get a list of rules and regulations.

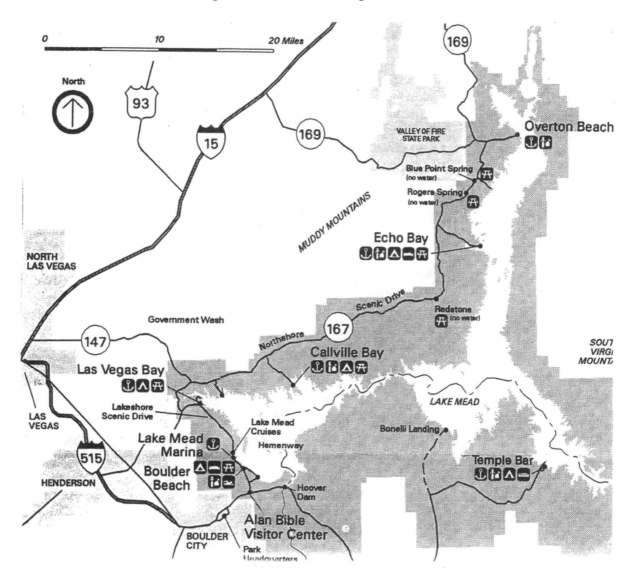

(Northern Section) Map courtesy of; Lake Mead National Recreational Area
(NOTE: Some of the features on this map have changed location or closed, check text for corrections)

ALAN BIBLE - LAKE MEAD VISITOR CENTER
Junction Highways 93 & 166
Open daily from 8:30 am – 4:30 pm (Closed Thanksgiving, Christmas & New Years days)
3 Miles west of Hoover Dam & 4 1/2 miles east of Boulder City
(702) 293-8920 www,nps.gov/lame
Mile 0

The Alan Bible Visitor Center has exhibits, a movie and current information about the area as well as books and maps available for sale. The center is an absolute "must" to enjoy the area. Note: The Lake Mead National Recreation Area resorts and attractions located east of the Colorado River and in Arizona are described in section b-4, page 49.

Between Lake Mead Marina and Valley of Fire State Park there are numerous attractions available to the traveler. Everything from hiking trails (some self-guiding) to geologic sites and picnic areas are found along the 50+ miles of the western shore of the lake.

We give most detail here to the attractions which are found between the Alan Bible Visitor Center and Highway 147 at Vegas Bay.

BOULDER BEACH ENTRANCE STATION
Mile ½
Pay your entrance fee here. This is also where you can pick up the maps and free information which you forgot to get while at the Visitor Center.

There are a variety of entrance and lake use fees available upon entrance to the National Recreation area. In addition to the standard 1 – 5 day pass there are annual passes with a discounted fee for any second vehicles.

There are also fees for vessel which include 1-5 day, annual or additional vessel fees.

ENTRANCE FOR HEMENWAY HARBOR & LAUNCH AREA, LAKE MEAD CRUISES
Mile 1

LAS VEGAS BOAT HARBOR MARINA
Located in Hemenway Harbor
Mile 1
Floating café & lounge, store, launch ramp, full service boating; renting, sales, parts & service, mooring & storage facilities
(702)293-3081, lasvegasboatharbor.com

LAKE MEAD CRUISES
Scheduled and charter boat cruises, & wedding/convention facilities, W/WO meals
P. O. Box 62465
Boulder City NV 89006
(702) 293-6180, info@lakemeadcruises.com

Photo: Courtesy of Lake Mead Cruises

Lake Mead Cruises offers a variety of Lake Mead excursions on two boats, including the famous *Desert Princess* which makes a variety of daily cruises, year-round, including views of Hoover Dam from Lake Mead.

Lake Mead Cruises also offers facilities totaling over 5,000 sq. ft. for large gatherings, such as conventions and receptions. These functions can be on the water, or in their shore facilities, or a combination of both.

BOULDER BEACH
Campground, RV's (Primitive, no hookups,) 150 yards to water, no boats
Mile 1.5

LAKE MEAD RESORT, MARINA & LODGE
Mile 3.5
Marina, NPS launch ramp, rent fish & ski boats, store, overnight mooring, café, lodge
(702) 293-3484, Reservations; (800) 752-9669 - www.sevencrown.com

The Lake Mead Marina is one of the more popular places on the lake. This marina offers a great number of attractions for the traveler. Everything from fishing tackle to general supplies are found in the general store.

The Lake Mead Marina also offers a coffee shop style restaurant on the dock. The launch ramp here is a busy place with people taking their boats in and out of the water.

SOME of the fish found along the docks at Lake Mead Resort and Marina!

One of the more popular attractions here are the large number of LARGE fish swarming the docks.

33 HOLE, 3 HOLE & ROCKY POINT OVERLOOKS
Covered picnic tables, barbeques & bathrooms
Mile 9.5

LAS VEGAS BAY ACCESS
MILE 11

JUNCTION HIGHWAY 147 SOUTH (To Henderson NV.)
Mile 11.3

JUNCTION HIGHWAY 147 & NORTHSHORE ROAD
MILE 13
From this point it is 20 miles west on Highway 147 to the I-15 in North Las Vegas (The West entrance gate is 6 miles west on Highway 147)
(The road going north along the lake now becomes "North Shore Road" at this point)

CONTINUING NORTH ALONG THE LAKE;

CALLVILLE BAY
Mile 23
Houseboat and personal boat rentals, auto & boat gas, launch ramp, slip rentals, boat repair, showers, laundry RV Park & campground, lounge & snack bar & lounge, store, (702) 565-8958, Reservations; (800) 255-5561

ECHO BAY
Mile 47
Motel, Restaurant & lounge, store, marina (with boat & auto gas), launch ramp, Laundry, Slip rental, houseboat, ski or fishing boat rentals, RV park w/full hookups, NPS campground, RV & boat dumps,
Motel (702) 394-4000

VALLEY OF FIRE,
EAST ENTRANCE TURN OFF
Highway 169 West
Mile 54

NOTE: This is a fee area and you must pay even to drive through it. It is worth the cost. Note: You may wish to travel through Valley of Fire and return to the turnoff or continue through the park and proceed on some 17 miles to I-15. (If you should elect to continue through the park to I-15 you will be 18 miles closer to Las Vegas and 18 miles further from Mesquite than if you should continue through the Moapa Valley on the other leg of Highway 169.)

SIDE TRIP
VALLEY OF FIRE STATE PARK
Hiking, climbing, camping (no reservations)
P.O. Box 515, Overton, NV 89040
(702) 397-2088, vof@mvdsl.com

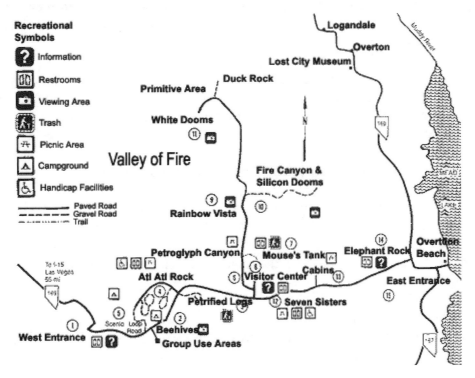

Map courtesy of Nevada State Parks

VALLEY OF FIRE VISITOR CENTER
5 Miles from the turn-off from Northshore Road

Make this an early stop upon entering the park. There is much to see and do here. With the staff's expertise and written information available there, it can make your trip more pleasant and you can travel better informed. The center is a Ranger Station that also offers books, film, slides and postcards.

As you travel through the park the fire colored sandstone formations you see were formed during the age of the dinosaurs and are some 125 to 150 million years old.

The Valley has many attractions in addition to the crimson colored rocks including petroglyphs, a silica dome, petrified wood and a great deal of history. From prehistoric times to the present, many people have used this valley, including a defiant Indian, who used it as a hideout in the 1890s.

OVERTON BEACH
Mile (Junction of Highways 167 & 169
Mile 56
Ranger Station- **Part time only,** public launch ramp, rest rooms, fish cleaning
(702) 394-4040

In 1864 Overton Beach became a steamboat port which was used by the Mormon Church to help in moving supplies to Salt Lake City. Eventually the port was complete with a landing, Post Office, corral, and warehouse.

The first attempts to get a steamboat this far up the Colorado River failed due to strong river currents and rapids at Black Canyon. In 1867 two steamboats, Esmeralda and Nina Tilden were equipped with steam winches and used iron rings which had been embedded in the cliffs to literally haul the craft up river.

The first load of supplies was delivered to the Overton warehouse in 1866.

In 1867 the U.S. Army arrived here and constructed Fort Callville. Due to the desolate location of the fort, it is reported that Fort Callville had the most desertions of any army stations in the area.

The completion of the transcontinental railway into Nevada in 1869 all but ended the riverboat traffic along the Colorado River.

In 1865, in order to grow cotton, the Mormons established St. Thomas at the junction of the Muddy and Virgin Rivers   In 1870 due to increasing taxes by the State of Nevada, all but one of the pioneering families, the Bonellis, returned to Utah.

Eventually some families did return and by 1910 the area was so productive that a railroad spur was run to St. Thomas.

Upon the completion of Hoover Dam, the waters of Lake Mead rose to the point where many of the buildings in St. Thomas were moved to higher ground.

Today, during periods of low water levels of Lake Mead, some of the remnants of what was once a small, but thriving, community reappears.

The National Park Service began concession development at Callville Bay in 1967.

THE MOAPA VALLEY/LOST CITY MUSEUM
MILE 62
Gas, Food & Lodging

The Moapa Valley is an oasis fed area rich in agriculture and is the home of the Clark County Fair. The valley is approximately 35 miles long and contains several different communities that in 1980 were combined into one community, Moapa Valley.

Mormon farmers first settled the valley in 1865. However when the boundary change moved the area from Utah to Nevada in 1871 the Mormons moved back into Utah. In the 1880s the Mormons returned and resettled in the valley.

THE LOST CITY MUSEUM OF ARCHAEOLOGY.
721 South Highway 169 (Moapa Valley Blvd.)
Overton, Nevada
(702) 397-2193
lostcity@comnett.net
Open daily 8:30 to 4:30 daily (closed Thanksgiving Day, Dec 25th & Jan. 1st)
Fee

In the Overton area is one of the most unique museums in Nevada. As the water built up behind the newly constructed dam, creating Lake Mead, Anasazi Indian sites were being threatened. In order to save and protect these artifacts, this museum was built by the National Park Service. In addition to the artifacts contained within the museum, replicas of the Anasazi dwellings themselves were created at the museum.

This Nevada State Museum is open, with the exception of major holidays, on a daily basis. Even the Museum's location is rich in history. The Museum is located on a part of Pueblo Grande de Nevada, an archaeological complex that dates back to the Anasazi Indians.

The displays start with the desert some 10,000 years ago and continue through the Mormon settlers of the 1860s.

In addition to displaying and interpreting numerous cultures that abounded in the area, the museum contains numerous artifacts inside. Outside, the grounds contain a recreated 7th century pit-house and a 10th century pueblo situated on their actual prehistoric foundations.

The name "Lost City" Museum? After the site was abandoned, it eroded and was buried or "lost." Lake Mead covered about 5 miles of the total 30-mile site area. (702) 397-2193

One of the "recreated" adobe houses at the Lost City Museum

JUNCTION HIGHWAY 169 & I-15 AT GLENDALE
MILE 74
Gas, Food & Lodging
(On I-15:Mesquite 29 miles north, Las Vegas 46 miles south)
Access to: Caliente, Pioche, Panaca & Cathedral Gorge State Park via Highway 169

Heading north on I-15 the country begins to green as we approach Mesquite. We will soon enter the Virgin River Recreational area. By taking Highway 170, which parallels I-15, we will better see this recreational area.

MESQUITE, NEVADA
Mile 103
All Services

Today Mesquite is a mixture of the old west and at the same time has a little of the grandiosity of Las Vegas. Mesquite is the home of older historic buildings and modern casinos and hotels sporting fountain filled lakes.

Like so many other Eastern Nevada cities, Mesquite began life as the result of Mormon expansion from neighboring Utah. Settlement was attempted in 1879 and again in 1887. Both times the settlers were forced out of the area by the flooding of the Virgin River. In 1894 one more attempt was made to farm the fertile but flood-prone Mesquite Flats. By the turn of the century the stubborn pioneers were beginning to reap a return from their efforts. Soon the area began to see more and more settlers arriving with the character to face the challenges found here.

The agriculture of this area has flourished ever since with not only crops but also livestock. Mesquite has long supplied substantial quantities of dairy products to rapidly growing Las Vegas. Mesquite's location near the border on the Interstate has been cause for the increase in the gaming industry. Today there are casino/resorts in mesquite that rival those in Las Vegas.

VIRGIN VALLEY HERITAGE MUSEUM
35 West Mesquite Blvd, Mesquite NV 89027
(702) 346-5705
Tues. – Sat. 10 am to 3 pm (1st & 3rd Weds. from 6 pm to 8 pm)
Mesquite's Desert Valley Museum at 35 West Mesquite Blvd. is located in one of two surviving facilities build by the National Youth Administration during 1941-42. This museum contains a variety of items from the ancient petroglyphs to early slot machines. Many of the items found in this historic building were donated by the docents themselves. The Docents have a great deal of inside knowledge about the area.

ACCESS TO SOUTHWESTERN UTAH/ZION NATIONAL PARK
PAGE 96 SECTION "E"

Some of the attractions found in Southwestern Utah are found beginning on Page 86, in Section "E' of this book.

It is 26 miles to St. George Utah from Mesquite, Nevada via I-15.

END OF SECTION B-2

TRIP B-3, EAST OF HOOVER DAM, DOWN ARIZONA HIGHWAY 93

ARIZONA HIGHWAY 93 FROM HOOVER DAM TO: TEMPLE BAR RESORT, WILLOW BEACH HARBOR, CHLORIDE, KINGMAN, GOLDROAD AND OATMAN, ARIZONA, AND A PORTION OF ROUTE 66

MILEGE SHOWN TO KINGMAN, ARIZONA IS FROM HOOVER DAM
(MAP PAGE 23)

ITEMS TO NOTE: 1. Arizona is in Central Time Zone and is 1 Hour Ahead of Nevada time, (except when Nevada & California are on daylight savings time)
2. Since 9-11 there can be delays in crossing Hoover Dam due to security reasons. Scheduled for completion in 2008, **The Hoover Dam Highway By-Pass** Bridge will decrease traffic on the dam.

WILLOW BEACH MARINA

14 Miles south of Hoover Dam to turnoff, 4 miles to Willow Beach
River trips, boat rentals & gas, launch ramp, convenient store & gift shop
(928)767-4747 – www.willowbeachharbor.com

Access to the Colorado River and the Black Canyon area is found here. This is also the upper end of Lake Mohave which extends down to the Davis Dam at Laughlin, Nevada.

This area of the Colorado River is in the Lake Mead National Recreation Area and is under the control of the National Park System.

There are restrictions on motorized boats from this point north towards Hoover Dam. These restrictions prohibit water skiing, wakeboarding and houseboats at anytime. Other motorized boats are prohibited on certain days (Check with the marina for the latest of these restrictions.)

This is also the termination of the raft portion of the Black Canyon/Willow Beach river adventures tour from just south of Hoover Dam.

Stripe Bass and Channel Catfish are caught here. At the same time the cliffs along the river, up to several hundred feet high are home to Big Horn Sheep and Blue Heron are also native to the area.

This is a unique way to explore an area, lots of wildlife along the shore and at the same time fishing can be good.

When construction began on Hoover Dam, workers were hauled up-river from Willow Beach to the dam site until roads could be built to the area where the dam was under construction.

TEMPLE BAR RESORT

19 Miles to turn-off, follow signs for an additional 28 miles.
Cabins, RV's, restaurant/lounge, ski & cruiser boat rentals, launch ramp, auto & boat fuel, slip rentals, gift shop/convenience store (minimum supplies) shower, laundry
(928)767-3211Reservations (800) 752-9669
P.O. Box 545, Temple Bar AZ, 86443
From Hoover Dam south on Highway 93 (Arizona side) 19 miles south to marker #19, follow signs for 28 miles.

Located in an area known for excellent fishing and with miles of smooth water for water skiing, Temple Bar's remoteness is one of its many assets.

SIDE TRIP
CHLORIDE, A GHOST TOWN, ALMOST
53 Miles South of Hoover Dam to Chloride Road **(County Road 125 east 4 miles)**
Gas, food, RV parks, camping, shopping

There are numerous ghost towns throughout the west and a large number of them live, or have died, in the state of Arizona, Chloride is somewhat unique, even in the "ghost town" category.

The famous "Chloride Murals"

The town of Chloride got started in1862. Activity here began in 1840's as the result of a silver strike; however hostilities with the Haulapai Indians slowed the mining activities. After a treaty with the Native Americans, Chloride soon became the site of some 75 mines. The Chloride Post Office, founded in 1862, is the oldest Post Office in Arizona still in operation. Numerous other metals were mined in the area after the initial silver discoveries.

In the 1960's a band of "Hippies" located in the hills around Chloride. During this time one of the band members, Roy Purcell, painted murals on rocks on the outskirts of town.

The murals are located south of town. Follow Tennessee Avenue to the south end of town and follow the signs, about 1 ½ miles.

As a note as you follow the short trail from the mural parking area to the Purcell murals, look to the left at the murals, petroglyphs, on the rocks which were created long before Purcell's.

Today Chloride offers the visitor the old bank, jail, train station, mines and mine shafts, numerous places to shop (jewelry, historic items and junk. There is also a convenience store, several restaurants, RV camping and several BLM campgrounds above town. On weekends the visitor might be witness to staged gunfights held "downtown." These mock fights might be done between men, or between women.

Chloride Chamber of Commerce
P.O. Box 268 Chloride, AZ 86431 (928) 565-2204, www.chloridearizona.com

JUNCTION HIGHWAY 68
Mile 72 (1 mile north of Kingman)
Access to Bullhead City, Arizona & Laughlin Nevada – 26 miles

KINGMAN, ARIZONA
Full services, Route 66 museum, Old Powerhouse attractions.
73 Miles south of Hoover Dam, (103 Miles south of Las Vegas) Highway 93

Kingman, Arizona is often referred to as the heart of Route 66. Kingman lies in the center of the longest remaining stretch of the historic "Mother Road" highway.

The Old Powerhouse, located at 120 West Route 66, (West Andy Devine Boulevard) was constructed in 1906 – 1907 and used as a powerhouse until 1940.

Today this historic building contains the local tourist information center along with numerous other tourist oriented attractions. The Old Powerhouse contains: Historic Route 66 Museum, Kingman Area Chamber of Commerce, an old west store, model railroad store, a gift shop, a diner, gallery and other attractions.

The Mohave Museum of History and Arts located, at 400 West Beale Street, contains the heritage of the area in maps, photos, manuscripts and documents.

HEADING WEST ON ROUTE 66 FROM KINGMAN TO OATMAN & AREAS WEST

GOLDROAD
23 Miles west of Kingman, Arizona on Route 66
No Services

The hills along Route 66 on the way from Kingman to Goldroad

Twenty three miles west of Kingman, Arizona lays the ruins of another turn of the century mining community, Goldroad. It is reported that Goldroad had its beginnings in 1899 as the result a large gold deposit found at that time. In 1942 the Powers War Act shut down mining. Goldroad then became an abandoned the town. The town had been constructed primarily of rock and adobe it looked like a town, when the tax assessor found it!

The then owner of the town-site was forced to dynamite the building in the town to avoid paying taxes based upon the value of the abandoned structures. But even that was not the final death for Goldroad. In 1992 the mine was sold and through improved mining techniques and the use of chemicals, the Gold Road Mine operated from 1995 through 1998. Then, a drop in gold prices once again forced the closure of the mine.

There is still gold in the mine and with further increase in gold prices it is highly likely that mining could resume. In the meantime, visitors have the opportunity to tour the inside of the gold mine, the Gold Road Mine Tours!

GOLD ROAD MINE TOURS - Fee
P.O. Box 869, Oatman, Arizona, 86433
(928) 768-1600 – FAX (928) 768-9588 www.goldroadmine.com

Guided tours of this historic mine which include black lighting of gold ore, demonstrations of actual mining tools, and a tour of the machine shop and being able to look down 300 feet. The mine tours are available from 10 am to 4 pm daily (except Thanksgiving, Christmas and New Years Day. The tour goes some 780 feet into the mine has been structured so there are no physical limitations for visitors. Even the tracks for the ore cars have been removed to make the tour wheelchair accessible. The tour lasts between 45 minutes and 1 hour. One of the highlights of this tour is passing 300 feet BELOW Route 66. As an added incentive, the temperature is always cool here!

This sign is located 300' below Route 66

OATMAN/ ARIZONA, A HISTORIC TOWN
27 Miles west of Kingman on Route 66 (2 ½ miles west of Gold Road)
Food, shopping, gun fights
In the foothills of the Black Mountains lies the historic community of Oatman, Arizona. Oatman's name comes from the name of a family which was attacked by the Apaches in 1851 with all of the members of the family being killed seriously wounded or held captive by the Indians for years.

The town was established around the turn of the century with the discovery of gold in the craggy mountains surrounding the town site. Today, the town offers a picture into the history of the area along with shops and other tourist attractions. Today "wild" Burros wander down the main street of town past the historic Oatman Hotel where Clark Gable and Carole Lombard honeymooned

On weekends and holidays the local gunfighters stage shoot-outs on the main street of town.

HEADING WEST FROM THE OATMAN AREA

There are *three western access roads* from the Oatman area. The two northerly roads will take you to Bullhead City area, via the first road which is partially paved and the second, which is paved all of the way to the east bank of the Colorado River some 6 miles south of the first road. The third road is Route 66.

Route 66 is accessed from the main drag through Oatman heading south.26 miles to the community of Topock. At Golden Shores, 20 miles south of Oatman on the east side of the roadway, there is a commemorative plaque to Route 66.

At a point just east of the Colorado River Route 66 is "covered" by I-40. The original Route 66 appears in several spots on the west side of the river in the town of Needles.

The original Route 66 bridge across the Colorado River still exists. The original bridge has a large arch and it is painted white. Today, the historic bridge is used to carry several gas lines across the Colorado River.

Route 66 is under I-40 until the off-ramp for Highway 95, North, 11 miles west of Needles. The section of Route 66 from that point, through the community of Goffs, to the access to the I-40 at Fenner is described on page 46 of this book.

Route 66 from Barstow to Oatman, Arizona is described in our book "Mojave Desert Windshield Adventuring. Included in that book are several realignments of the historic roadway.

The bridge in the foreground is the original Route 66 bridge, now carrying gas lines. The newer I-40 bridge is in the background

SECTION B-4 ROUTE 95 BOULDER CITY NEVADA TO NEEDLES CALIFORNIA
(Southbound)
From the Junction of Highways 93/95 at Railroad Pass to Interstate 40
84 Miles to I-40 westbound, 80 miles to I-40 eastbound

From its northern terminus 6 miles east of Henderson, State Route 95, a four and two lane highway, follows the Piute Valley to I-40, at a point west of Needles, California.

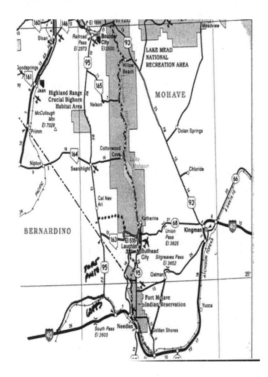

THIS SECTION INCLUDES THE FOLLOWING SIDETRIPS:

Map courtesy of Nevada Department of Transportation

ELDORADO CANYON – STATE HIGHWAY 165
Mile 10 (East)

SIDE TRIP
NELSON (10 MILES) (no services) & **TECHATTICUP MINE** (12 MILES): tours, canoe and kayak rentals, **COLORADO RIVER ACCESS**. (17 Miles) **NOTE:** Hand boat launches only.

Located just an hour south of the glitz and glamour of Las Vegas is a canyon which once provided millions in gold and silver, exceeded Las Vegas in population and used steamboats as the main mode of transportation.

Unlike most of Nevada this portion of the state was initially explored by boat! The first recorded exploration of the Colorado River by steamboat was made during the winter of 1857-58. George Alonzo Johnson who is credited with the discovery and naming of Eldorado Canyon captained the steamboat. The river trip from Yuma, Arizona to Eldorado was some 365 miles. The port at Eldorado was soon to become the busiest Nevada port along the Colorado River.

The *Cochan,* an early steamboat on the Colorado River

Prior to the building of the numerous dams along the Colorado River the river was traveled by steamboats to points both above and below Eldorado Canyon. The steamers not only hauled the ore down to Yuma, Arizona or through to the Sea of Cortez, they also brought supplies to the settlements along the river. The construction of Davis Dam and the creation of Lake Mohave "drowned" the steamer landing at Eldorado Canyon.

Eldorado Canyon was the site of one of the biggest mining booms in Nevada. It began around 1859 with the discovery of gold and silver. During the 1860's many of the miners were Civil War deserters. The mining activity was about five miles above the Colorado River. Soon a number of large mines began operation. Wall Street, Morning Star, January and Techatticup were some of the more productive. (The Techatticup is the mine that is open for tours and was named in an unusual manner. The name Techatticup came from an Indian guide who when asking for food using the Paiute word for hungry: "Tecahenga" and "to-sup" meaning flour or bread.)

From 1863 into the 1890's a mill was located at the base of the canyon on the Colorado River. After that time the ore was removed from the mines and was hauled the five miles down the canyon to the Colorado River for shipment by steamboat. During this period the population here was greater than Las Vegas.

The history of Techatticup is one of much violence, most of which was the result of disputes over mining claims in the area. Stories have it that the ghost of a murdered claim-jumper still haunts one of the mines. One of the more "infamous" violent characters during this era was a renegade Indian, Queho, who murdered a woman here in 1919. She was reputed to be his 23rd victim. Mummified remains, found in a cave near Hoover Dam in 1940, were identified as those of Queho.

There is evidence showing that the early Spanish explorers had visited Eldorado Canyon as far back as the 1700's in their search for gold. During the 1880's, a time of heavy mining in the canyon, a group of Mexicans suddenly appeared in the canyon with an old Spanish map of Eldorado Canyon and highlighted on the map was the very area which was currently yielding the highest-grade ore in the canyon. The mining in Eldorado Canyon continued into the 1940's when all mining except that vital to the war effort was halted. During the productive life of the Eldorado Canyon mines, millions of dollars in gold and silver ore was processed from her mines.

TECHATTICUP
ELDORADO CANYON MINE TOURS & COLORADO RIVER TOURS, Inc
Mine Tours, Canoe & kayak rentals, historic buildings and articles
RESERVATIONS ARE REQUIRED!
(702) 291-0026, HC Box 440, Nelson, NV 89046
Eldoaradocanyonmintours.com or www.coloradorivertour.com E-mail: bobbiewerly@yahoo.com

Twelve miles from Highway 95 and two miles down the canyon from the community of Nelson, at a wide spot in the road, stands Techatticup. The multi-story barn on the north side of the highway and the huge wooden vats on the south side of the roadway make the historic site impossible to miss. One of the unique features found in Techatticup are guided tours of the mine.

Access to the mine itself is with a guide only. Since 3 or more people are required for a mine tour, reservations are recommended. Individuals and groups are often combined. Mine tours are from approximately 9:15 AM to 2:15 PM, no later tours at anytime. The Techatticup is carried on the mine registry as an "operating mine" and is subject to all of the safety requirements in place for any mine.

Inside the Techatticup mine

The trip through the mine is not a long or hard walk. There is no climbing involved and the entire tour is "user friendly" with no extremes. The mine, which is now a combination of the Techatticup and the Savage mines, contains some three miles of tunnels in levels 600 feet in depth. While the tour covers only a small portion of the total mine, it tells a rather complete story of mining from the last century through the middle of this century.

Once one is a short distance into the mine the temperature drops to a comfortable 68 degrees.

A "replica" of Dead Ed found in Techatticup Mine

The mine today is complete with many of the tools and equipment used in the mining operations from before the turn of the century until mining operations stopped in the 1940s. It was not hard to visualize the hardships endured by the miners who worked here. There were between 15 and 90 men working in the mine during the peak years of operation.

"Dead Ed" died in while working in the mine in 1905 as the result of his own mistake.

Ed tamped powder into a blasting hole with a metal rod instead of his wooden one. His real name was unknown and he was buried in a tailings pile outside of the 200-foot entrance.

This is the same entrance used today for tours. The skeleton in the mine is not that of "Dead Ed," however the replica placed as nearly as possible to the position where "Ed" met his end.

The flooding and then the damming of the Colorado River and economic changes halted steamboat operations along the river so the milling operations were moved from their original site at the river to the site of the mines.

The large vats located outside of the mine were used to extract the gold from the crushed ore by the use of cyanide. Prior to being placed into the vats, the ore was crushed by what was thought to be a 10-stamp mill.

In addition to the mine at Techatticup the Werlys also offer kayak and canoe rental and/or tours on the Colorado River. Six people are required for the guided kayak tours. No motorized boats are either rented or used on the tours. Also, the Werlys offer a combination mine tour and/or a kayak/canoe tour

SEARCHLIGHT NEVADA
State Route 164, EAST; Cottonwood Cove/Lake Mojave. WEST; Nipton/I-15
Mile 36
All services including lodging
Highway 164 West to I-15 is described in another section.
According to information acquired at the Searchlight Museum this rustic little crossroads town might have acquired its name as the results of a miner's exclamation that "if there was any gold here, you would need a searchlight to find it."

Searchlight has an excellent restaurant in the Nugget Casino. The Nugget appears to be a focal point for the Searchlight area with bulletin boards, containing local information, at both the front and rear entrances. There are several "convenience stores" in Searchlight.

SEARCHLIGHT MUSEUM
200 Michael Wendell Way (Highway 164 East,) Searchlight, NV (702) 297-1682
Monday through Friday, 1- 5 p.m. & Saturday, 9 a.m. - 1 p.m. Admission is free.

This unique little museum is located approximately 3/4 of a mile east of the intersection of 164 and 95, on the way to Cottonwood Cove, at 200 North Michael Wendell Highway in the Searchlight Community Center.

This museum focuses on the 100 year history of this community, with emphases on mining. Mining was, after all, the main cause of the "birth" of the community of Seachlight. There have also been several residents of Searchlight who have achieved notoriety. Two of these personalities are Mouri Rose, 2-time Indianapolis 500 race winner and the noted song writer and arraigner, Scott Joplin.

SIDE TRIP
(EAST OF SEARCHLIGHT)
COTTONWOOD COVE

12 Miles East of Searchlight on Lake Mojave (Lake Mead National Recreation Area)
Café, motel, store, marina, ski, fishing, deck cruiser & houseboat rentals, launch ramp, auto &
boat gas, showers, laundry, RV site & NPS camping.
12 Miles East of Highway 95
P.O. Box 1000, Cottonwood Cove, NV 89046
(702)297-1464, Reservations (800)255-5561

Located near the northern end of Lake Mojave in an area which features both excellent fishing and generally smooth waters for water skiing, Cottonwood Cove offers full services.

The motel offers beachfront rooms for those who would prefer to sleep on dry land in addition to an RV park and Campground.

Lake Mojave offers 240 miles of shoreline and is bordered on the south by Davis Dam. Davis Dam is located at the northern end of Laughlin, Nevada.

WEST OF SEARCHLIGHT
NIPTON STATION

20.5 Miles West of Searchlight
(I-15, 10 MILES)
(760) 856-2335, www.nipton,com
HCI BOX 357, Nipton, CA 92364
Trading Post w/jewelry etc, books & information, sandwiches etc.
Restaurant, Bed & breakfast, RV hookups & camping, Jacuzzi, no gasoline.
NOTE: Mojave National Preserve & alternate routes to So. Ca. on Page 47

Historic Nipton Station was established in 1885 and is located at the junction of California State Highway 164 and the Union Pacific Railroad in the Ivanpah Valley. Both I-15 and the casinos and hotels at the Nevada State Line, 11 miles north across the Ivanpah Dry Lake are generally clearly visible from this "outpost" in the middle of the desert.

The general store at Nipton contains food, Indian jewelry and a very complete selection of maps and books on the desert, and friendly information.

Adjacent to the general store is a Bed & Breakfast, built in the period of 1904-1910.

The store at Nipton Station

The hotel features sweeping views of the mountains and the desert from the front porch or from Jacuzzi hot tubs.

There are RV hookups and campsites with hot showers and flush toilets. The Nipton Station is open 7 days a week from 8 a.m. to 6 p.m. For hotel reservations and store information call (760) 856-2335.

The Nipton Station Hotel

Nipton Station has undergone many changes and much remodeling in the past several years.   The third hot tub is now in place and there are now four "eco" lodges (electrified tents with fireplaces) awaiting the traveler.   The front patio has been enclosed and cooled and it, along with the restaurant have become the "The Whistle stop Oasis," a café serving wine and beer.   Chef Bill Sarbello, originally from New York, but more recently a practicing chef in the Virgin Islands presents a menu that should satisfy anyone tastes!

CHRISTMAS TREE PASS/GRAPEVINE CANYON
Mile 48
SIDE TRIP
(NOTE: The only facilities are porta-potties at the entrance to Grapevine Canyon)

This "scenic" route is located on the East Side of Route 95 and in the southwest corner of the Lake Mead Recreational Area. This 15 mile long maintained dirt road winds its way from Nevada State Route 95 five miles north of the junction of State Route 163 to State Route 163 five miles west of Laughlin Nevada.

As it winds its way through the Newberry Mountains, in addition to many spectacular views, this route offers a variety of plants and rock formations as it changes elevation. There are numerous petroglyphs sites in this area.

In the springtime this road is lined by a variety of wildflowers and cacti in bloom. Several streams meander across the road. At the upper elevations, numerous unusual rock formations abound. 5,600+ foot high Spirit Mountain is just to the north of the pass.

Once the site of numerous camping areas, camping is now restricted in this area and should be investigated by contacting the Lake Mojave Rangers before setting up camp.

We found the drive easiest by going from State Highway 95 east to Highway 163 because of the terrain. Even though the road is maintained, it is dirt, and caution should be used especially after rainstorms.

Grapevine Canyon access is located off of Christmas Tree Pass Road, three miles from the junction of Highway 163. Grapevine Canyon is known as the largest and most prolific petroglyphs site in Nevada. From the parking area, it is a ¾ mile hike to the site.

How did Christmas Tree Pass get its name? The "story" is that in years past the trees along the road through the pass would be "decorated" for the holidays, decorated with lots of things, many of which were "unmentionables!" That practice is now illegal and the rangers will site the tree "decorators".

HIGHWAY 163 JUNCTION
To: Laughlin, Nevada.- Bullhead City, Katherine's Landing, Oatman & Goldroad, Arizona
Mile 54

ATTRACTIONS:
(CHRISTMAS TREE PASS/GRAPEVINE CANYON Mile 15, road on north side of highway. NOTE; there is NO LEFT TURN FROM EASTBOUND 163 to these attractions, make a right turn just east of the turn-off, then a U turn & go back up the hill.)
DAVIS DAM ACCESS Mile 18.
LAUGHLIN, right turn at the signal at the bottom of the hill. Mile 19)
BULLHEAD CITY, cross the bridge, right turn (Oatman & Kingman Arizona access)
LAKE MOHAVE RESORT, cross bridge, turn left on road #68, right on spur road to Katherine landing.

SIDE TRIPS – SOUTH FROM HIGHWAY 163
LAUGHLIN, NEVADA
Gas, food, lodging, gaming, water sports & river tours

Twenty miles to the east of this desolate intersection is the oasis of Laughlin, Nevada and Bullhead City, Arizona which line opposite banks of the Colorado River. Davis Dam, just above these 2 towns, controls the flow of the river as it heads toward the Sea of Cortez.

Full services are located in the Laughlin/Bullhead City area, including numerous casinos and hotels in Laughlin.

Laughlin offers numerous shows, special events and fine dining opportunities but generally at a cost less than found some 90 miles to the north.

Laughlin from the Bullhead City side of the Colorado River

The majority of the Laughlin resorts are located along the west bank of the Colorado River. Having river access allows the use of water taxis to take patrons from resort to resort and to the parking lots across the river. These water taxis do charge a fee. Several of the resorts offer beaches and personal watercraft, "Skidoo" type, for rent. There is also a promenade along the riverbank, giving access to the majority of the waterfront resorts.

There are several river tours available in the Laughlin area. The majority of these tours are of the immediate Laughlin area. There is one major exception.

A JET BOAT SIDE TRIP FROM LAUGHLIN TO LONDON BRIDGE
6 HOURS (Round Trip)
58 MILES BY BOAT

Since 1998 tourists have been whisked along the scenic Colorado River from Laughlin to the historic London Bridge located at Lake Havasu City, Arizona. Using high speed, 40 mile per hour, jet boats the passengers skim across the top of the unusual river and through the unforgettably beautiful Topock Gorge.

The two boats are run by the owner-operators; Joe and Jenny Fitch.

These high-speed boats depart for their "fun runs" from Laughlin at around 10 am, after picking up passengers from the various hotels' docks.

In addition to many waterfront homes along the riverbank there are numerous metal structures. These structures enable various entities to pump water from the river. So much water is pumped from the Colorado, that by the time the river reaches the Sea of Cortez, it is barely a trickle.

One of the more interesting features found along the river is in the area where four bridges cross it. One of the bridges is supported by a large arch and has several gas lines on it. This is the original bridge which used to carry historic Route 66 across the river.

This unusual rock lives along the river in Topoc Gorge

Once past the bridges the river begins its journey into scenic Topock Gorge. This area can only be visited by boat, or "hardy hikers." Towering cliffs and multi-colored rock formations line the river. There are also petroglyphs along the shore. The gorge teems with wildlife; from numerous hawks to hard to spot, wild burros, bobcats, and big horn sheep among others.

Upon leaving Topock Gorge, the river enters Lake Havasu, which is 24 miles long and up to 4 miles wide.

Leaving Lake Havasu, our boat turns up Bridgewater Channel where, in the distance stands London Bridge. London Bridge was brought to Lake Havasu City in 1968, in pieces. Installation of the bridge was completed in 1970.

Our boat ties up at the dock at the base of London Bridge where the passengers are given 2 hours to eat, walk the bridge and visit shops in the area, prior to returning to Laughlin.

London Bridge, the jet boat's destination

It has been our experience that not only is this boat ride a fun and scenic way to travel, it also can be faster than driving the two lane roadways from Laughlin to London bridge!

LONDON JET
PMB 508* 1650 Casino Drive,
Laughlin, NV 89029
Toll Free; (888) 505-3545 or Local (702) 298-5498
www.jetboattour.com

EAST OF THE COLORADO RIVER (ACROSS THE COLORADO RIVER BRIDGE)
SOUTHERN SECTION OF THE LAKE MOHAVE RECREATION AREA
BULLHEAD CITY
OATMAN AND KINGMAN ACCESS
(Across the Colorado River Bridge at Laughlin)

Arizona highway 68, a continuation of Nevada Highway 163 on the east side of the Colorado River, goes eastward 25 miles to Arizona Highway 93 at a point 4 miles north of Kingman Arizona. Arizona Highway 95 goes south from the intersection of Arizona 68 through Bullhead City with access to Oatman, Goldroad and Kingman Arizona (Pages 37 & 38) via Route 66 from Oatman/Goldroad and access to I-40 – 40 Miles.

LAKE MOHAVE RESORT AT KATHERINE LANDING
(7+Miles north of Bullhead City/Laughlin ARIZONA SIDE)
2690 E. Katherine Spur, Bullhead City, AZ 86429
(928)754-3245, Hotel Reservations: (800) 752-9669
Full marina: launch ramp, houseboat, small boat & wave runner rentals,
Boat/auto gas, boat repair, store, motel, restaurant, RV Park, campground.

Located on the eastern (Arizona) side of Lake Mohave, Katherine Landing offers full services for the water enthusiast.

Katherine Landing took its name from a mine which was located north-east of the existing marina. The mine's name was originally Catherine and began production in the mid-1860's. In 1904 the Catherine mine was closed down.

In 1919 the Catherine Mine, now known as the Katherine Mine began a re-birth period as more developing was being done. (The name change was probably done for legal reasons.)

The mine operated, this time, until 1929 when the Katherine Gold Mining Company declared bankruptcy.

During the 1930s the Katherine Mine was re-opened and operated until April 15, 1943, when it was closed by the War Production Board. The Catherine/Katherine mine was never as productive as the numerous satellite mines which grew up around it.

Once, there were numerous mines in the area are now divided by Lake Mohave. A few remnants remain in the area of this once productive mining area. (Some are under the waters of Lake Mohave in the Katherine Landing area.)

BULLHEAD CITY
East Bank of the Colorado River, south of the bridge.
Gas, food, lodging, full services

Bullhead City, Arizona is partially a bedroom community for the people who work in the resorts and other businesses across the river in Laughlin. Bullhead City is also popular as a retirement area.

ACCESS TO OATMAN & GOLDROAD
(OATMAN & GOLDROAD ARE DESCRIBED IN DETAIL ON PAGE 38)

There are three roads from the west going to the Oatman area. #1. From Arizona Highway 95 at a point 4 ½ miles south of the junction of Highway 68, there is a turnoff to Bullhead Community Hospital. This route, while the shortest and most scenic, eventually turns into a dirt road and is not advised in wet weather and might be a better "return route" from Oatman.

The second access road, completely paved is off of Highway 95, 16 miles south of the junction of Highway 68 and is Highway CR 153, Oatman Road. It is 13.5 miles into Oatman from Highway 68.

The third route is via Route 66 from I-40 (A long way from the Bullhead City area.)

BACK ON I-95 SOUTHBOUND
FORT PIUTE TURN OFF
Mile 67

Continuing south on Highway 40 at mile marker post 75 on the west-side of the highway is the turn off to Fort Piute. (NOT SIGNED) NOTE: HIGH VEHICLE CLEARANCE IS RECOMMENDED. Directions to Fort Piute are found on the following page.

FORT PIUTE

If one was asked to conjure up a picture of a desert oasis, it is not unlikely that the result would be on the order of Piute Creek at the location of Fort Piute. Here, in the middle of the desert, for about a half-mile this underground creek comes above ground. This "oasis" has been the source of life for many animals, Native Americans and travelers for centuries.

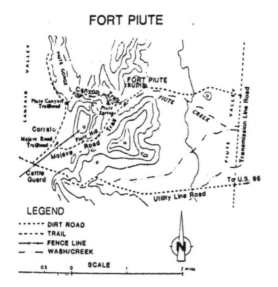

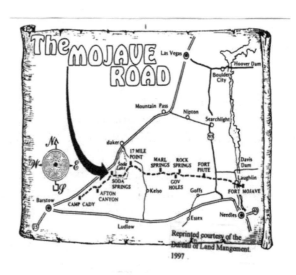

Map to Fort Piute (turn rt. on transmission line road)
Access map courtesy of Bureau of Land Management

This map shows all of the Mojave Road outposts
Map courtesy of the Bureau of Land Management

Though short lived as a military reservation (1866-1867), the ruins of the "Outpost at Piute Creek" as it was eventually known are quite recognizable. Initially the outpost was named "Fort Beale" after Edward Beale who had led camels through the area. It was renamed Fort Piute in 1866. Fort Piute was one of the stopping points along the Mojave Road which extended from the Colorado River to just east of Barstow. (All the outposts along the Mojave Road are described in "Mojave Desert, Windshield Adventuring" ISBN#0-9664055-8-7)

A portion of the remaining walls at Ft. Piute

A plaque, in the wall, showing the layout of Ft. Piute (or Pahute)

Much of the outpost/fort has been washed away by water coming down the washes located behind it. In 1983 the BLM stabilized the remaining walls of the blockhouse by cementing the inside to prevent further erosion. There is a plaque at the blockhouse site that shows the layout of the original structures.

There is much more here than just the remains of the outpost. Piute Canyon itself is the destination of many visitors to the area. Westward from the site of the outpost are petroglyphs and other remains of the past. Bird watching is also popular in the area.

There are two hiking trails into the canyon from the west side of the canyon. Both of these trails require about a two-hour hike, each way. The trailheads are located in the Lanfair Valley approximately 10 miles from the intersection of Lanfair and Cedar Canyon Road.

GETTING THERE: Located west of CALIFORNIA Highway 95. 6 1/2 miles south of Highway 163 and 10 miles north of Goffs Road go west at mile marker post 75. (NOTE: There are two dirt roads approximately 1 mile apart, the southernmost one is the easiest access.) Go west for 7 miles to a power line road where you will go right (north) for 1.4 miles to the 2nd road on your left. It is 2 miles up this extremely rocky, high vehicle clearance road.

CAMP IBIS (site)
Mile 73
Monument/entrance, East Side of Highway 95 1 mile north of Arrowhead Junction

The area east of Arrowhead Junction, a major training site during World War II, was called Camp Ibis. During World War II the deserts of the southwest were used as numerous training facilities. Camp Ibis was certainly one of the largest.

As one drives through the remnants of this historic site little remains from the tens of thousands of soldiers who trained here from 1942 to 1944 in preparation of joining General Patton in the conquest of Europe. The desert is gradually reclaiming the site as it continually washes out the roads and the improvements made for the camp. No buildings remain here but close examination will disclose the rocks that were used to mark the areas were tents and other temporary improvements once stood. While it is possible to enter the area of the camp with most any vehicle, 4-wheel drive in strongly recommended. Take care as the "camp" roads have really deteriorated.

ARROWHEAD JUNCTION
Mile 74

One mile south of the marker for Camp Ibis and immediately after crossing the railroad track is Arrowhead Junction, which marks the intersection of Goffs Road, an extension of Route 66. The roadway going straight-ahead, and curving to the left, is still Highway 95 but additionally is a remnant of Route 66 East, The National Trails Highway. Turing right after crossing the railroad is Route 66 West, and a shorter way to I-40 West. If headed EAST on I-40, it is shorter to continue south on Highway 95 at Arrowhead Junction as it is 6 miles to I-40.

Heading WEST on Goff Road, AKA National Trails Highway-Route 66, it is 14 miles to the community of Goffs, (No Services) and a total of 24 miles to I-40. From Arrowhead Junction the historic Route 66 goes westward through historic Goffs. Periodically there have been various services offered here, however at this writing there are no services in Goffs. After crossing the railroad track at the outskirts of Goffs, our road goes to the left, heading west. Going straight ahead 1/8 mile is the headquarters for the *Friends of the Mojave Road.*

The recently restored Goff's schoolhouse

The group known as *The Friends of the Mojave Road.* headed by *Dennis Casebier* has done much to attempt to restore many of the historic areas of the eastern Mojave including the *Mojave Road.* One of the major restoration projects of Mr. Casebier and the Friends of the Mojave Road has been the restoration of the historic *Goffs School House* located in Goffs. The Goff's schoolhouse has had quite a history since the County of San Bernardino built it in 1914 when it served as "the school" for 1,000 square miles. From 1954 to 1982 it was neglected and suffered much vandalism. As the result of Casebier and the Friends of the Mojave Road's efforts the schoolhouse has recently been placed on the National Register of Historic Places. Dennis Casebier, 37198 Landfair Road, Essex, CA 92332.

Ten miles west of Goffs, Goff's Road, (Route 66) accesses Interstate 40 at Fenner (Gas & Food, Supplies & highway access) from where it sweeps south towards Essex and Amboy.

THE MOJAVE NATIONAL PRESERVE &
ALTERNATE ROUTES TO SOUTHERN CALIFORNIA

MOJAVE NATIONAL PRESERVE

Information Centers: Kelso Depot, intersection of Kelbaker and Kelso-Cima Road, Hole in the Wall and Barstow, 2701 Barstow Road, Barstow, CA 92311, (760) 252-6101 www,nps.gov/moja

Afton Canyon with the Mojave Riverbed
(dry in summer) in the foreground

We have continually and actively explored the 1.6 million-acre Mojave Preserve since the early 1990's and have never been bored by its wonders. From camping amid the pinions and junipers at Mid Hills campground to exploring the outposts located along the Mojave Road to the marbled canyon called Afton we have found new adventures on every venture into the preserve.

Located between the I-15 & the I-40 and between Barstow and California Highway 95, the preserve offers mountains, deserts, sand dunes and a variety of wildlife and vegetation. There are posted wilderness areas which are closed to all motorized vehicles, but there are still many areas to explore by vehicle. It is recommended that exploration off of paved roads be done either by checking condition with rangers prior or with 4 wheel drive. There is no "off roading" allowed within the preserve.

While there are three campgrounds available, there are also motels & hotels available in cities and towns surrounding the preserve. It is always a good idea to travel with plenty of water, and maybe a little extra food. Also make sure your car is in good operating condition. Some of the unpaved roads shown on maps of the preserve should only be attempted in high clearance 4 wheel drive vehicles. Check with the rangers on current conditions.

During the mid 1860's one of the major roads west was the Mojave Road. The Mojave Road started at Fort Mojave, on the east bank on the Colorado River and extended 138 miles to Camp Cady located at a point just east of what is now Barstow, California. Spaced at intervals along the way, there were six outposts which had water.

Traveling the entire original Mojave Road today can only be accomplished by multiple 4 WD vehicles with high clearance. There are portions of the road which are passable only by winching.

It is possible to visit all of these outposts by accessing them from other roadways. Access to Fort Piute (Pah-ute) is described on page 44. Access to all of the Mojave Road outposts are found in our publication, "*Mojave Desert Windshield Adventures.*"

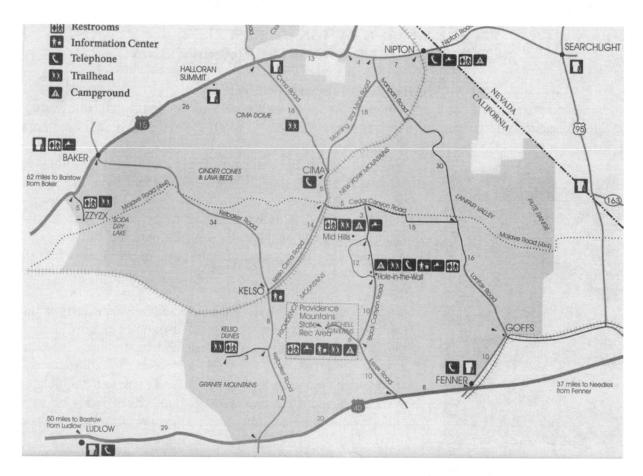

MOJAVE NATIONAL PRESERVE
Map courtesy of Western National Parks Association

ALTERNATE ROUTES TO SOUTHERN CALIFORNIA
Nipton station to Barstow via the Mojave National Preserve and I-40
(A summation of the route is at the end of this section.)

If you are tired of the 90+ mile per hour kamikaze drivers on the I-15 you might want to try what we found to be a more relaxing, and certainly a more scenic route going towards the west.

FROM NIPTON STATION: Go west 7 miles to Ivanpah Road (I-15 is another 3 miles west of this junction.) Turn left, south on Ivanpah Road for 3 miles then turn right on Morning Star Mine Road. Continue on Morning Star Mine Road for 15 miles to the area known as Cima. Cima contains a post office/general store. The store stocks limited supplies and is not always open.

At Cima continue south at the beginning of Kelso Cima Road for 19 miles to Kelso. (Note, at mile 5 is Cedar Canyon Road to your left and a dirt road to the right. This is one of the crossing points of the historic Mojave Road. The plaque on the right side commemorates this historic route.

54

FREMONT STREET EXPERIENCE – PAGE 13
Thousands are entertained nightly by this unique attraction

STRIP'S NEW YORK ROLLER COASTER - PAGE 15

ALONG THE ROAD TO CHINA RANCH - PAGE 63

STORM CLOUDS OVER DOWNTOWN LAS VEGAS - PAGE 13

ABANDONED MINE, OUTSIDE OF GOLDFIELD NEVADA – PAGE 84

SPRINGS AT ASH MEADOWS NATIONAL WILDFIFE REFUGE – PAGE 89

COOK BANK BUILDING, RHYOLITE NEVADA – PAGE 93

TOPOC GORGE - PAGE 47

HEART OF TITUS CANYON – PAGE 94

DEATH VALLEY NATIVE – PAGE 70

OFF THE BEATEN PATH" DEATH VALLEY NATIONAL PARK – PAGE 68

WHITE TIGERS LIVE IN THE HABITAT AT THE MIRAGE HOTEL- PAGE 17

RED ROCK CANYON CONSERVATION AREA, WITHIN SIGHT OF THE "STRIP" - PAGE 58

HEADED FOR I-15, LEAVING VALLEY OF FIRE ON HIGHWAY 169 - PAGE 31

COLORADO RIVER "TRAFFIC" LAUGHLIN, NEVADA - PAGE 46

KOLOB CANYON - PAGE 102

COLORS FOUND IN ZION NATIONAL PARK – Page 99

"LOW TIDE" AT LAKE MEAD DURING DROUGHT – Page 27

At mile 19 is the Kelso Depot Visitor Center and Ranger Station, a "must see." Past the Kelso Depot turn left on Kelbaker Road. Turning right will take you north 36 miles to the I-15 at Baker.

After turning left on Kelbaker Road you should notice large sand dunes to your right, the Kelso Dunes. There is an access road to the dunes 8 miles south of Kelso. Shortly after passing the dunes the road begins a gentle climb between the Granite Mountains on the right and the Providence Mountains on the left. Big horn sheep are occasionally spotted along the hillsides here.

TheI-40 freeway is 18 miles south of Kelso Depot. From the junction of Kelbaker Road and I-40 it is 28 miles to Ludlow which has full services and 49 miles from Ludlow to Barstow.

SUMMATION:

From Nipton Station; west 7 miles, left on Morning Star Road south 15 miles, to Cima. Kelso-Cima road (straight ahead) 19 miles to Kelso. At Kelso turn left south on Kelbaker Road 18 miles south to I-40. West on I-40; 28 miles to Ludlow, 77 miles to Barstow.

The Mojave National Preserve's Kelso Visitor Center at the intersection of Kelbaker and Kelso-Cima Roads

SECTION C WEST OF LAS VEGAS

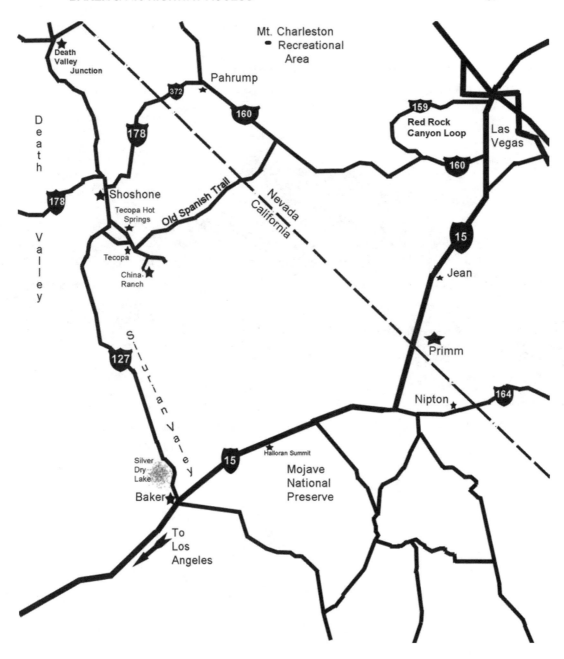

THE RED ROCK CANYON LOOP – SECTION C-1

MAP COURTESY OF BLM

SECTION C-1 THE RED ROCK CANYON LOOP
Las Vegas and return, 40 miles round trip
Highway 159 (Charleston Blvd.) through Red Rock Canyon to Highway 160 & return
(The mileage shown to the various destinations is from the entrance to the scenic drive.)

Heading west on Highway 159, Charleston Boulevard, the rapid growth of Las Vegas becomes quite evident. More and more construction is underway both for residential and commercial buildings.

After entering the Conservation Area boundary there is a sign warning not to feed the burros. Common sense doesn't always prevail with some people in regard to these "cute" animals. This is sometimes evidenced by parents picking their hurt children out of the dust after placing them on one of these wild animals in order to take a picture or someone needing medical attention after being bitten or kicked by one of them.

RED ROCK CANYON NATIONAL CONSERVATION AREA
Mile 18 Fee area – Closes at dusk
Hiking, camping*, climbing, biking, books & gifts
HCR 33, Box 5500, Las Vegas, NV 89124
(702) 515-5350, www.redrockcanyonlv.org

If looking westward from many of the Las Vegas hotel rooms you can see tall cliffs into view, cliffs with a wide red horizontal stripe across the center of them, what you are looking at is most likely a portion of Red Rock Canyon. These are the cliffs which run along the western portion of this spectacular area. These cliffs are but a sampling of what awaits the visitor to this unique area.

The Conservation Area offers 198,000 acres of recreational scenic opportunities for the visitor. A thirteen mile drive circles a portion of the Conservation Area and gives access to the majority of the attractions as well as numerous trailheads. There are 30 miles of hiking trails within the Conservation Area.

The Red Rock Canyon Visitor Center

The visitor center is open daily, year round, and contains a museum exhibits and a book store/gift shop in addition to postings of naturalist-guided walks, programs and talks in addition to hiking /maps. The monthly activities include: nature walks, hikes, kids activities and evening programs offered by the Red Rock Canyon Interpretive Association.

For a schedule of education-based activities; www.redrockcanyonlv.org. or (702) 515-5367

The Red Rock Canyon National Conservation Area, RRCNA, is managed by the Bureau of Land Management with the co-operation of the Red Rock Canyon Interpretive Association.

Camping at Red Rock is restricted to September through May and is done on a first come- first served basis. No wood or fuel is available at the campground. (No wood fires allowed in the park)

SPRING MOUNTAIN RANCH STATE PARK
(West of Highway 159, 5 miles south of Red Rock Canyon Park, 6 miles north of Highway 160)
INFORMATION: BOX 124, BLUE DIAMOND, NV. 89004
(702) 875-4141, smrrangers@parks.nv.gov

In 1829 Red Rock Canyon Trail became an alternate route to the original Spanish Trail not only because it was shorter but also and probably, more importantly, because it had water.

There are 52 springs located in the valley which encompasses not only Spring Mountain State Park but also what is now Red Rock Canyon National Conservation Area. Six of the springs are located on the 520 acre Spring Mountain Ranch.

In 1850 the Red Rock Canyon Trail became a part of the Mormon Trail to California which was replaced by the railroad in 1905.

Spring Mountain State Park Barn. (Photo courtesy of Nevada State Parks)

The 1860s saw a one room shack at the ranch location and it is widely believed that the area was used to hide horses and other livestock which had been stolen in California and moved east on the Mormon trail from the missions and ranchos in California.

The site had been periodically farmed during the early 1860s but it wasn't until 1876 that the 360 acres of the land was formally filed on and became the Sand Stone Ranch. This homestead was registered to James Wilson and George Anderson. In 1906 Wilson's two sons inherited the ranch property and used it as a cattle ranch.

In 1919 the ranch had a large mortgage on it which was foreclosed on. A family friend acquired the ranch and gave the two brothers a life estate to the two cabins on the property. In 1959 the life estate ceased with the death of the last of the two brothers.

Between 1919 and 1944 several owners of the property made various improvements to it and used the acreage for different agricultural purposes.

In 1944 Chester Lauck ("Lum" of the "Lum & Abner" radio show) acquired the property and began construction of the main house that exists today. Lauck was a "gentleman rancher" and used the property primarily for vacation purposes. Lauck named the "spread" the Bar Nothing Ranch. There was much entertaining done here during this time. Lauck added the irrigation system that is in use today.

Vera Krupp, the ex-wife of German munitions industrialist Alfried Krupp, purchased the ranch in 1955 to use as her prime residence. Mrs. Krupp added the swimming pool and west wing to the house. Incidentally should you visit the house you might ask the docent to show you the secret passage that Mrs. Krupp had built between her room and the South Wing.

One evening in 1959, while Mrs. Krupp and her ranch hands were eating dinner, three men rode up on horseback. These were robbers who tied up Mrs. Krupp and stole her large and expensive jewelry collection before riding off into the sunset!

Subsequently the entire collection was recovered and the thieves punished. An interesting note is that one of the jewels stolen and recovered was a 33+-carat diamond. This diamond was purchased at auction in 1967 following Mrs. Krupp's death and subsequently given by Richard Burton to Elizabeth Taylor.

Mrs. Krupp had sold the ranch to the Howard Hughes Corporation in 1967. There is no record of Howard Hughes ever using the ranch even though was used as a corporate weekend entertaining facility.

In 1972 Fletcher Jones and William Murphy, two businessmen from Southern California, purchased the ranch with the idea of developing the land for townhouses. Public outcry resulted in the two businessmen offering to sell the property to the Nevada Division of State Parks. The sale was finalized in 1974.

Located at the foot of the Wilson Cliffs, adjacent to Red Rock Canyon Natural Conservation area, the ranch is a 520 acre oasis in the heart of the desert. There are numerous tree shaded picnicking spots in the park

The living history program at this park brings the past to life and gives visitors to glimpse life as it was through out the history of the ranch. This costumed re-enactment's have since 1992 depicted the lives of the early settlers in the area.

The Park is open daily for daylight use and the ranch house itself is open with guided tours Friday through Monday and on state holidays. The ranch house has a gift shop. There is a per-vehicle entrance fee.

BONNIE SPRINGS RANCH/MOTEL/OLD NEVADA
(West of Hwy. 159, 5.5 miles south of Red Rock Canyon Park, 5 miles north of Hwy. 160)
1 Gunfighter Lane, Blue Diamond, NV. 89004
(702) 875-4191 – info@bonniespringds.com
Motel- (702) 875-4400 – reservations@bonniesprings.com

While having been built recently, Old Nevada is an accurate reconstruction of a historic town, no false fronts here, in which the entire family can literally step back into history and enjoy. The town part does have an admission charge.

The "hitchin" chapel at Bonnie Springs Ranch

In 1843 Bonnie Springs Ranch was built primarily as a stopover for the wagon trains traveling the Spanish Trail. In 1846 General Fremont stopped here to gear up for his trip to California. This area was one of the last "wet" spots prior to crossing Death Valley.

In the early 1950's Al and Bonnie Levinson, both of whom had developed a love for the old west, began the project of recreating the town as it would have existed back in the late 1800's.

After extensive study of the history of that period in time, the re-creation of the mining town "Old Nevada" began in the 1970's.

Old Nevada is complete with a saloon, an opera house (with live performances), and a wax museum (which takes the visitor not only back in history but also into the workings of an 1880 mine).

There is an authentic wedding chapel (in which weddings can and are still performed) and an original 1902 operational 5 stamp mill. The town is complete with museums, several stores, a tavern, U.S. Post Office, restaurant, and several shops to hide out in during the recreated gun fights or public hangings that occur on the town's main street. There is also railroad that one can ride on weekends and holidays.

How about a breakfast horseback ride through the desert? Yes, horses are available for rent and guides are available.

Today, in addition to the "town" of Old Nevada, there is a motel with themed rooms. The motel offers a selection of rooms, and prices, including "Luv Tub" rooms, with no kids allowed in these particular rooms. There are several eating establishments, including a dinner house, complemented with a cocktail lounge. Shuttle service is available from Las Vegas.

* * * * * * * *

Some 7 1/2 miles south of the scenic drive entrance is the town of Blue Diamond. The town can be seen on the hillside to the west of the highway.

At the junction of Highway 160 heading east will take you back to the I-15 just south of McCarran Airport via the Blue Diamond Highway.

SECTION C-2 LAS VEGAS TO BAKER VIA THE SCENIC ROUTE
I-15 SOUTH OF VEGAS TO I-15 BAKER CALIFORNIA (137 Miles)
MAP PAGE 56

From the I-15 highway, approximately 4 miles south of Tropicana Boulevard, take Blue Diamond Road, Highway 160, west.

JUNCTION, RED ROCK CANYON LOOP, SOUTHERN END
Junction Highway 159
Mile 10.5

MOUNT POTOSI
Mile 18
No services, Nevada State Marker

Approximately 7 1/2 miles to the west of the intersection of Highway 159, on the south side of the highway, is a place of note, Mount Potosi. Mount Potosi Mine was the first mine in Nevada to be closed down.

This mine was opened in 1856 in order to obtain lead for shot for the Mormon settlement at Las Vegas. Approximately 9,000 pounds of lead were taken from the mine before it was shut down in the following year, 1857. The reason the mine was shut down? There was too much silver in the lead, and the shot would not hold together when fired from a weapon.

Several times after the closure of the mine, different interests reopened it. Once in 1861 and then again in 1905 and as late as World War I the area was being mined again, this time for zinc.

Highway 160 from the junction of Highway 159 travels through Cottonwood valley and past Mountain Springs. This route pretty much approximates the route of the Old Spanish Trail, which ran from Santa Fe, New Mexico to Los Angeles.

Mount Potosi was also the site of the World War II plane crash which ended the life of Carol Lumbard, the movie actress who was Clark Gable's wife.

After passing the Mount Potosi turn off the highway climbs to the picturesque community of Mountain Springs. Just west of the community is the Mountain Springs Summit, altitude; 5493 feet.

From the summit our roadway drops down into a wide sweeping plain.

OLD SPANISH TRAIL ACCESS ROAD
(AN ALTERNATE ROUTE TO THE SHOSHONE AREA & BAKER)
Mile 37 (15 miles SOUTH of Pahrump)
(37 miles to access to Highway 127, (Baker Roadway) 8 miles south of Shoshone,)
(No services for 44 miles until Shoshone. This route bypasses Pahrump)
(The Old Spanish Trail was a historic route used in the 1800's that wound its way from Santa Fe, New Mexico through Utah and eventually through the Cajon Pass to Los Angeles)

This paved roadway crosses a fairly desolate plain for 21 miles then ascends a short distance up a windy road to the summit of Emigrant Pass.

After crossing over the summit there is a tremendous change in the scenery, especially in spring and summer. Along the road are large pockets of greenery, a far cry from the almost barren topography found on the other side of the pass.

This area contains pockets of springs, the majority of which are hot which accounts for the greenery.

CHINA RANCH (SIDE TRIP)
Mile 70.50
Date Ranch, gift shop, Bed and Breakfast
China Ranch P.O. Box 14 Tecopa, CA 92384, (760) www.chinaranch.com.

Thirty three miles from the turnoff from Highway 160 there is a paved road to the south, left. One mile and one eighth (1 1/8) from that intersection is Furnace Creek Road, a roadway to the right (south.) It is about 2.5 miles down this roadway to the China Ranch Date Farm Store. The route from the Old Spanish Trail is generally signed.

The road into the valley containing China Ranch, winds through a spectacular canyon, and is accessible by all vehicles in good weather

In the 1880's a Chinese man, who remains nameless, planted fruits and vegetables in this oasis in order to service the local mining camps with fresh fruits and vegetables, hence the name Chinaman's Ranch. It was in the 1920's that the first date grove was planted here and today this family run operation offers the traveler a variety of not only home grown dates but also baked goods and hand gifts.

The China Ranch Date Farm Oasis. Photo courtesy of China Ranch

Located within the oasis at China Ranch is the Ranch House Inn, a unique bed and breakfast which operates from the end of September through the end of May. This unique experience offers numerous amenities to their guests and includes breakfast and optional lunch and dinners. Nick & Cynthia Kienitz, Ranch House Inn, P.O. Box 14, Tecopa, CA 92389. (760) 852- 4358, www.ranchhouseinn.com.

TECOPA/TECOPA HOT SPRINGS LOOP
Mile 72
No Services

Returning to the Old Spanish Trail we will be 1 ½ miles east of the community of Tecopa. The only services in Tecopa is the Post Office which has been is service since 1877.

Tecopa was named for a Piute Indian chief, who had befriended early settlers, it is located in an area covered by trees and other greenery. This "oasis" can be a welcome spot in the heat of the desert. Tecopa was a site where the borax coming from Death Valley was crystallized as the higher altitude made it cooler in summer...

To the West Side of the now closed trading post is s dirt road that is the entrance to Amargosa Canyon. The canyon itself is closed to motor vehicles. The dirt road gives an insight into the mining operations that kept this settlement functioning for so many years.

Going straight ahead on the road through Tecopa for 4 miles will take us to the junction of Highway 127, 48 miles north of Baker and the I-15.

TECOPA HOT SPRINGS: Taking a right turn on the first paved road east of Tecopa will take you into the area known as Tecopa Hot Springs. For countless centuries these springs have been in almost constant use.

The hot springs in this area are unusual. Even though the springs are at a temperature of 116 degrees and highly mineralized, there are none of the odors which are quite often a part of the hot springs experience.

DELIGHT'S HOT SPRINGS RESORT: is located two blocks north of the stop sign, at the windmill sign. This historic resort is being upgraded and now offers private hot spring rooms, complete with showers. Delight's is available for day use in addition to offering cabins, with kitchens and RV facilities for overnight visitors.

The office is the original schoolhouse from Death Valley.

Information: Delight's Hot Springs Resort, 368 Hot Springs Rd., Tecopa Hot Springs, CA 92389 delightshotspringsresort.com, (800) 928-8808,

By continuing on the loop road we will be 5 miles from Highway 127 and a total of 10 miles south of the town of Shoshone offering full services.

END OF LOOP TRIP ON OLD SPANISH TRAIL
* * * * *

RETURNING TO OUR ORIGINAL ROUTE, NORTH ON HIGHWAY 160

From the turn off to the Old Spanish Road it is approximately 15 ½ miles to the junction of Highway 372 (which becomes Highway 178 in California.) The junction is located in the center of Pahrump, Nevada.

PAHRUMP, NEVADA
Mile 52 (26 miles from Shoshone)
All Services
Pahrump Chamber of Commerce: P.O. Box 42, Pahrump, NV 89041 (775) 727-5800

Just 8 miles from the California Border and at an altitude of 2695 feet, this community offers a milder climate than the deserts around the valley in which it is located. The name Pahrump is from a Piute Indian word that interprets to mean "water rock" or "Place where big waters flow." Pahrump has numerous attractions including golf courses, an Olympic sized swimming pool, a 7-acre park, casinos and nightclubs.

Leaving Pahrump it is a long uphill grade as our highway heads towards the California Border. Upon entering California, our highway becomes Highway 78.

Access to **ASH MEADOWS NATIONAL WILDLIFE REFUGE** from the Pahrump area is found on Page 88.

SHOSHONE
MILE 79
All Services

This old mining town "built by borax", was a stop on the T&T Railroad, and has survived the virtual demise of mining in the area due to tourism. Shoshone has become a "hub" for this area of the desert. This oasis of green surrounded by the harsh Mojave Desert and the mountains of the Greenwater and Resting Springs ranges have offered relief to the traveler for many years.

One unusual feature to be found in Shoshone are the "Castles in Clay."

These old homes of miner's are located in Dublin Gulch, approximately 1/4 west of the intersection of Highway 127 and Highway 178 east, which is at the southern end of Shoshone. These are unusual desert "apartments" certainly worth the short trip up the dirt road.

The Castles in Clay are located west of the intersection of Highways. 78 & 127

On both sides of this canyon are old miner's homes that were dug out of hills. Complete with chimneys, porches and multi-rooms these "apartments" were inhabited rent-free by miners and others as late as 1991. The "clay castles" are open for exploration.

Shoshone has all services including a local museum. Where else would you find a bar called, "The Crowbar"?

From Shoshone our route takes Highway 127 **South**. (For **Death Valley National Park**, page 68, go **north** on Highway 127, 2 miles to Highway 178 west, 76 Miles west to Furnace Creek Ranch.)

Five miles south of Shoshone on Highway 127 is the junction of **Tecopa Hot Springs access road**. (This area is described on page 64.) The southern loop of the Tecopa Hot Springs road access is 3 miles south of this road.

As the road crosses the valley, you will be able to see what was once a large prehistoric lake, Lake Tecopa. Today the area almost seems to still be prehistoric. Large sandstone sculptures rise from the ground surrounded by areas of green vegetation. Hot springs abound in an area which is bordered by two-mile high mountains to the east

As the roadway leaves the valley and climbs towards 2,090 foot high Ibex pass located in the colorful and rugged Saddle Peak Hills. From the summit the road descends into the Silurian Valley.

From this point Highway 127 follows the course of the historic Tonopah and Tidewater Railroad through the Silurian Valley.

The Tonopah and Tidewater Railroad was initially intended to run directly from Tonopah Nevada to Santa Monica, California. From 1909 until 1940 the line ran from Goldfield, Nevada to Ludlow, California, roughly the middle portion of its intended route. For all but five years of its existence the line ran at a loss. Yet the line was so important to the mines in the area, especially the companies owned by "Borax" Smith, that he subsidized the cost of operating the line from his other operations.

In 1943 the ties and rails along the line were salvaged. The rails were used in the war effort and the ties, so it is said, were used in the construction of the El Rancho Motel in Barstow, Furnace Creek Inn in Death Valley and The Apple Valley Inn in Victorville.

North along Highway 127, the berm that supported the railroad roadbed can be seen running parallel to the highway. In order to preserve the berm, driving a vehicle on the berm has been CLOSED, EXCEPT from the site of Riggs north to the site of Sperry. A four-wheel drive vehicle should be used in most of the areas off of the highway including the berm in the authorized section

DUMONT DUNES
22 Miles south of Shoshone
This area is designated for the use of off road vehicles that quite often can be seen charging across the starkly colored dunes.

HARRY WADE EXIT ROUTE
27 Miles south of Shoshone
BEFORE TAKING THIS ROUTE CHECK WITH RANGERS IN DEATH VALLEY ON ROAD CONDITION (760) 786-3200! !

The plaque on the West Side of the highway at the Harry Wade exit commemorates the spot where, in 1849, Harry Wade saved his family after leaving the ill-fated party of '49ers in Death Valley. He found this junction with the Old Spanish Trail, and was able to head southwest to the Cajon Pass.

Today this dirt road heads into the southeast corner on Death Valley National Park and to several abandoned mines as it joins Highway 178 at several spots inside the park.

ABANDONED TOWN SITES

From this point southward there were three major town sites, all of which are off of the highway and require 4 wheel drive and have totally disappeared with the exception of a concrete block or two. These towns were located along the Tonopah and Tidewater Rail Road and serviced the mines which were in production in this area.

Shortly before the town of Baker the West Side of this highway becomes dominated by "Silver Lake", a huge dry lake. When the "T & T" railroad was initially built the tracks went across this dry lake on their way north. Some 8 1/2 miles north of Baker on the Eastside of the highway is what once was the location of the town of Silver Lake. This is the second site of the town of Silver Lake! Initially both the railroad and the town were located in the "dry" lakebed, however flooding forced their being moved to the other side of the highway.

BAKER & I-15 – END OF SECTION C-2
Mile 58 from Shoshone, Mile 137 from I-15 Las Vegas
All services

Residents of Red Rock National Conservation Area

SECTION C-3 DEATH VALLEY NATIONAL PARK

Death Valley National Park

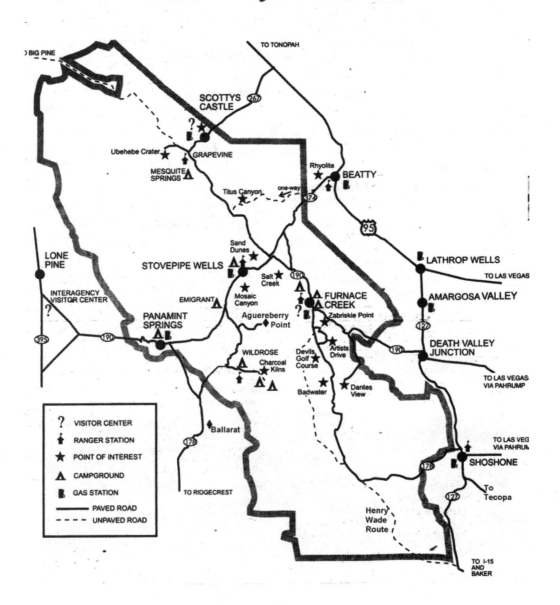

Map courtesy of the National Park Service & Death Valley Natural History Association

DEATH VALLEY NATIONAL PARK
Gas, food, supplies, gift shops, lodging RV & camping
P.O. Box 579, Death Valley, CA 92328
(760) 786-3200, www.nps.gov/deva
Daily weather report & Road conditions: (760) 786-3200
National Park Service Reservations: (800) 365-2267
Camping reservations: www.nps.gov
Hotel reservations: Furnace Creek Inn & Ranch, Stovepipe Wells (760) 786-2345

Larger than some states, this huge national park contains 3,336,000 acres with some 3,000,000 of these acres in wilderness.

This is a land that features varieties: temperatures which reach well over 120 degrees, nearly a thousand types of plants and wildflowers, the lowest spot on the continent (Badwater Basin) in sight of the highest spot in the continental United States (Mount Whitney) seen from Aguereberry Point. Intermingled with the park's natural resources are a multitude of remnants from the area's mining background.

There are five highways and Titus Canyon Road, a "scenic" unpaved roadway, giving access into the main portion of the park from the east. Additionally, there are two paved roads giving access to the park from the west.

The roads from the east that enter the valley are: Highway 267 at Scotty's Castle Page 105; Highway 374 from Beatty and/or Titus Canyon Page 114 as an alternate, Page 114; Highway 190 from Death Valley Junction, Page 109; and Highway 178 just north of Shoshone, Page 66. The "scenic" route, Harry Wade Exit Route, Page 66, accessible from Highway 127, is 27 miles north of Baker and 16 miles south of the southern end of the Tecopa Hot Springs loop and is a primitive road. Traveling the Harry Wade route should be done by high clearance vehicles and **only after checking with the NPS road conditions. The information phone number is shown above.**

Highway 190 is an entrance road from the west. It is 104 miles from the Visitor Center located at the junction of Highways 136 (136 becomes 190 at a point 18 miles east of Highway 395) and 395, four miles south of Lone Pine. Wildrose Canyon Road **(a steep winding road which is restricted to vehicles under 25' long and 9' in width)** via Highway 178, from Ridgecrest and Trona (Page 77) is also a western entrance to the park.

Sandstone cliffs in Towne Pass along Wildrose Canyon Road

There is access to the north end of the park via *Big Pine Road* which is mostly unpaved and should be used only *after checking with the NPS road conditions phone number shown above.* Access to this road is from Highway 266 one mile east of Highway 395 a mile north Big Pine California. From Nevada Highway 95 access is via Nevada Highway 266, which becomes Highway 266 at the California Border. This road is 83 miles from the turnoff from Highway 168 to Scotty' Castle.

Death Valley is a fee area. Fees may be paid at Stovepipe Wells or at the Visitor's Center at Furnace Creek. Additionally, there are 15 automated machines throughout the park to pay the fee.

Much of Death Valley's history involves the famed 20 mule team borax teams of earlier days

Old mines, mills and mining towns and roads are found throughout the area. This is a dream location whether you are a historian, geologist or botanist.

Detailed maps are available, free of charge, at the visitor registration centers to help make your visit more enjoyable AND SAFER! People still die due to ignoring conditions here! NOTE: The most common cause of death within the park is from single car rollovers.

MAIN (EASTERN PORTION) OF THE PARK
This portion includes attractions located east of Stovepipe Wells
Attractions accessible from Highway 190, west of Stovepipe Wells, Page 74

Seeing Death Valley is not a one-day affair. The attractions and features of this park are not only plentiful and varied, but are generally located many miles apart. The majority of these attractions are accessible via well-maintained roads

Death Valley offers many opportunities to get away and head of on numerous back roads, many of which require 4 X 4 and/or high clearance vehicles. It is however, against park regulations to leave marked roads and it is also advisable to check road conditions with a park ranger or, online at www.nps.gov/deva. Check the front page, "Morning Report."

It is also advisable to check in and out with the rangers if your trip involves remote camping and/or traveling. Make sure to check on camping restrictions and rules for remote areas.

Supplies, restaurants, gift shops, and a complete information center are located at Furnace Creek and Stovepipe Wells. Restaurants, lodging and gifts will be found at Furnace Creek Inn. There are numerous improved and unimproved campgrounds and RV sites located throughout the park.

There is a multitude of material and information available at the Visitor's Center located at Furnace Creek. It is not our intent to provide the reader with a full itinerary of what to see and do in the park, rather we can "whet the interest" in sharing some of the attractions with you. The museum and visitors center at Furnace Creek also offers a slide show every 30 minutes which gives a good orientation on the valley.

There are ranger tours and talks scheduled at regular times during the high season; mid October through mid May, with current information available at the information desk in the center.

Harmony Borax Works is located 1 mile north of the visitor center and represents a significant part of the history of Death Valley. This was one of the major sources of Borax in the area and a starting place for the 165 mile trip to Mojave by the famous twenty mule team wagons. A visit to **The Borax Museum** located at Furnace Creek Ranch is a great source for the history of Borax mining in the valley.

Dante's View is located above Badwater and offers a spectacular view of the Badwater area. Dante's view is accessible from highway 190 by taking the 13.2-mile access road 11 miles south of Furnace Creek. It is well signed as are most of the major attractions located within the park. This road is restricted to vehicles with a total length of less than 25 feet.

Artist's Drive gives the visitor a spectacular series of many different colors that are found here in the desert. This short one-way loop drive also has a restriction of vehicles which are less than 25' in length. The colors are more brilliant here in the late afternoon.

Death Valley Scotty's Castle is more than just a castle in the desert; actually it is located at an oasis and surrounded by trees. Built in the 1920's at a cost in excess of $2.5 million dollars it was inhabited by a story telling, cowboy, miner, publicity-seeking "friend" of the castle's REAL owner. The true owner of the castle was Albert Johnson, a Chicago millionaire who had become entranced by his friend Walter Scott's tales of secret mines and riches in the area. Death Valley Scotty soon had everyone convinced that the castle was his!

The interior of Scotty's Castle is shown only during guided tours that are conducted daily between 9 AM & PM. There is a fee for these tours. Call for exact tour times as they do change.

Ubehebe Crater is located approximately 8 miles from Death Valley Scotty's Castle. This 2,400 foot diameter crater was created by a volcanic eruption 1,000 to 2,000 years ago. The crater is located within a volcanic field and is surrounded by smaller, older volcanoes. The area features an eerie atmosphere, but is well worth the trip.

Badwater is located near the southern end of the valley itself and is the lowest spot accessible by car in the park. At 279.8 feet below sea level it is only surpassed by several areas 3 to 4 miles away which are 282 feet below sea level, making them the lowest spots in the western hemisphere. While at Badwater turn and look above the parking area and high upon the cliff you will see the sign that marks sea level!

Badwater, desolation defined

There are so many unusual and exciting locations to visit in the park that it would probably take a book larger than this to do them all justice. One of the things that we attempt to do is to visit the park in the spring when the wildflowers are in bloom. It gives a whole different meaning to the word "desert." On one of our trips through the park we were treated to wildflowers peaking through a light and late snow on several of the passes.

WESTERN SECTION OF THE PARK
SECTION A Emigrant Canyon Road attractions
Aguerberry Point, Eureka Mine, Wildrose Kilns
SECTION B Panamint Valley attractions & alternate routes to Southern California, Page 77.

SECTION A
Highway 190, 8 miles west of Stovepipe Wells to Emigrant Canyon Road

NOTE: Many maps will show access roads to attractions, attractions and roads which are no longer there! If you have a high clearance 4 wheel drive vehicle (with a winch) you might be able to reach some of them. Check with Park Rangers before attempting side trips – there is NO off-roading allowed in Death Valley National Park.

WILDROSE CANYON
LIMITED ACCESS: VEHICLES OVER 25' LONG OR 9' WIDE PROHIBITED
(SIGNED)
Wildrose Canyon is a scenic winding and primitive road that drops steeply down the west face of the Panamint Mountains to Panamint Valley from an altitude of some 5,500 feet. The road is

passable by any automobile or other vehicle within the length and width limits (25' long & 9' wide) and certainly worth the trip. Heading down towards the valley after entering a narrow canyon with occasional springs and mine shafts the road passes sandstone cliffs then drops into Panamint Valley, enters a as it climbs the 9 3/4 miles to *Emigrant Canyon Junction.*

EUREKA MINE AGUEREBERRY POINT& AGUEREBERRY CAMP
Turnoff Mile 12

Approximately 2 miles from the junction of Emigrant Road is a road running right (west) to the Eureka Mine and Aguereberry Camp. The information at the site states that Jean Pierre "Pete" Aguereberry who had been a Basque shepherd turned prospector, and "Shorty" Harris, a character of "dubious" character, hit pay dirt here and began a mining operation.

Eventually they had a falling out and split the claim and each mined a separate portion of the claim. Pete Aguereberry lived here until the time of his death in 1941. Today this site is still in excellent condition, even to the tracks leading into the lower mine entrance and several out buildings built of stone, worth the side trip. Continuing 4 miles past the Eureka Mine the road terminates at Aguereberry Point. The road out to the point is rough but passable with any automobile.

One of the old mines in the Aguerberry area

AGUEREBERRY POINT

"One of the most panoramic views that can be experienced with both feet on the ground" best describes this spot. From a height of 6,500 feet one looks down on Badwater, the lowest spot in the United States at 280 feet below sea level! Much of Death Valley lies at your feet. By turning around, you will be looking at Mount Whitney, the highest point in the continental United States.

To the left of the sign the lighter area at the foot of the far mountains is Badwater, elevation 280' **BELOW** sea level

Returning to Emigrant Canyon Road it is 9 ½ miles south to Wildrose Kilns

WILDROSE KILNS

At the Emigrant Canyon Junction at Wildrose Campgrounds turn right for 9 miles and the climb up the valley to Wildrose Kilns.

These ten massive structures, 30' to 32' in diameter by an average of 25 1/2' high, were constructed in 1877 to manufacture charcoal needed in the processing of bullion at the nearby mining centers both in the Panamints and the Argus Ranges.

At the height of their operation each of the "beehive" kilns produced 35 cords in 17 to 19 days. It is not known exactly how long the kilns were actually in use but it appears that they were last used sometime in 1879.

During the 1930's the CCC affected limited repairs on the kilns. In 1971 the kilns were re-built by a group of Navajo experts from Arizona. Today it is still possible to smell the resin creosote within the giant kilns.

Don't miss the view of the High Sierra looking back down the valley from the kilns.

Returning to Emigrant Canyon Road it is 9 miles to Panamint Valley Road

SECTION B, PANAMINT VALLEY, PANAMINT MOUNTAINS, WILDROSE CANYON

The Desert Protection Act that was passed in 1994 increased the area of Death Valley National Park to where it presently extends further into the Panamint Mountains and into Panamint Valley in areas.

This area abounds with old mining claims, towns and "tales". Much gold, silver, lead & copper has been taken out of the area in the past. Presently at a spot mid way between *Ballarat & The Barker Ranch* (connected with the infamous Manson Family) recently a huge mine has been blasting and cyaniding gold out of the western face of the Panamints.

PANAMINT SPRINGS RESORT
Highway 190, 30 miles west of Stovepipe Wells,
15 miles north of Wildrose Canyon & 2 miles west on Highway 190
Gas, food, supplies, lodging, camping /RVs, convention facilities.
Reservations & information: (775) 482-7680, http.//www.deathvalley.com/
P. O. BOX 395 RIDGECREST, CA. 93556 (775) 482-7680 www.deathvalley.com

Panamint Springs overlooks the northern end of The Panamint Valley and the Panamint Dunes from its location on the eastern slope of the Darwin Hills. Located mid-way between the town of Lone Pine and Stovepipe Wells in Death Valley National Park, Panamint Springs is a great jumping off place for adventures in the Panamint area.

Panamint Springs consists of a motel, campground/RV park, restaurant, mini mart and gas station. The motel rooms are small but clean with individual baths including showers. The stories of the actual springs at Panamint Springs vary, depending upon who tells the tale. Some claim the springs were active as recently as the turn of the century. Others insist that the springs have not been active in the area for some 400 to 500 years. Today, all of the greenery in the area is irrigated.

It is rumored that the initial owner of Panamint Spring was the niece of William Cody who started the resort a stopping spot on the road to Death Valley in 1937. In 1945 the building that now houses the office and restaurant burnt down and subsequently rebuilt.

Facilities: Gas & propane fuel, mini mart, 14 unit motel and campground with hot showers, R. V. spots (with & without hookups), a quality restaurant, knowledgeable tourist information, trees, outstanding views of the desert & an unimproved airstrip. Panamint Springs is also available for day use and for conferences.

DARWIN FALLS

A waterfall in the middle of the desert? That's right, in fact if you can find the trail you can see not only one 40-foot waterfall you can climb to view the upper Darwin Fall.

The turnoff to Darwin Falls is located south west of Highway 190 just 1 mile west of Panamint Springs Resort. Some 2 1/4 miles up this dirt road is the signed turn off to the Darwin Falls trailhead that is 1/4 mile up the side road. (Past the Darwin Falls turnoff, it is a four-wheel drive only road. It ends up Darwin (a ghost town) some 6 miles past the falls.

The hike to the falls is about a mile over an increasingly harder trail that winds back and forth over a stream. There are several boulder climbs and other obstacles. The streambed is filled with trees and bulrushes and lined with granite walls, a fairly tough but scenic hike. The Darwin Falls area is an area of critical concern so please heed the anti-pollution requests.

ALTERNATE ROUTES BACK TO CIVILIZATION FROM PANAMINT VALLEY

ROUTE "A" HIGHWAY 190 TO HIGHWAY 395, VIA OLANCHA OR LONE PINE
Highway 395 via Highway 190 at Olancha = 48 miles
Highway 395 via Highway 190 & 136 at Lone Pine = 51 miles (21 miles north of Olancha)
(Mileage if from the intersection of Highways 190 & 178, Panamint Valley Road)

After passing Panamint Springs and the Darwin Falls access road, Highway 190 begins a steep climb up from Panamint Valley to the summit of the Argus Range. Near the summit is **Father Crowley Point.** The point is named for Father Crowley, known as the "Padre of the Desert," who gave extensive help to those affected by the draining of Owens Lake by the city of Los Angeles. The summit offers an excellent view of Rainbow Canyon and into the north end of Panamint Valley.

Thirty three miles west of Panamint Valley road is the junction of Highways 190 and 136, near the southeast corner of Owens Lake. Turning **LEFT ON HIGHWAY 190** will take you 15 miles to the junction of Highway 395 at **Olancha,** gas, food, lodging and supplies. Olancha is 21 miles south of Lone Pine, which is a much larger town.

At the intersection of Highway 190 and 136 by **going straight ahead on Highway 136** you will be 18 miles south of Highway 395 at the Visitor Information Center which is **4 miles south of Lone Pine** which offers complete services. As a note; this area and its attractions are described in greater detail in our publication, Mojave Desert Windshield Adventures, ISBN#0-9664055-8-7.

ROUTE "B' PANAMINT VALLEY ROAD, HIGHWAY 178, SOUTH TO HIGHWAY 395 THROUGH TRONA & RIDGECREST
Trona, full services 31 miles
Ridgecrest, full services 56 miles
Highway 395 (west of Ridgecrest) 66 miles

Panamint Valley is a place of contrasts. The mountains and hills on both sides of the valley were once alive with mines and mill sites. Access to these historic sites is QUITE LIMITED as most of the roads have washed out. As a matter of interest, the Wildrose charcoal kilns on page 74 were built to service the processing of the minerals mined in this area.

As a contrast, this valley has become a "playground" for the F-18s and other naval aircraft from the Naval Air Weapons Station, China Lake located just to the west. We have been "buzzed" and "played with" by high speed aircraft on numerous occasions as we traveled through Panamint Valley.

Just south of the intersection of Panamint Valley Road and Wildrose Canyon Road is a road to the east. This is Indian Ranch Road, a "back way" access to Ballarat. As the road turns southward it passes through a green, almost marsh like area, and a welcome sight after the dry valley. Note; this road could be hazardous after rainstorms.

BALLARAT AREA
23 Miles south of Highway 190, 3 ½ miles east of Highway 178
NO SERVICES, NO PHONE
(SIGNED)

There is a commemorative marker and sign leading to the ghost town. Ballarat can be seen across *Panamint Dry Lake* at the base of the Panamint Mountains.

One of the historic structures found in Ballarat

Named for a gold district in Australia, this town was founded in 1897 as a supply center for the mining communities located above the town in the Panamint Mountains. At the turn of the century *Ballarat* boasted a population of 400 people, a 2-story hotel, 7 saloons & 2 houses of ill repute. The former jail had been converted into a gift shop.

The wildlife in this area includes big horn sheep and wild burros. Occasionally, someone lures some of the wild burros out of the hills to eat food that has been left for them.

Today Ballarat is a camping/RV area located among some of the still standing adobe ruins of the original town. Camping here is primitive with no hookups. Showers are available at an additional charge. BRING YOUR OWN DRINKING WATER OR BE PREPARED TO BUY IT THROUGHOUT THE ENTIRE VALLEY. The water in the valley is not purified. NO GAS, TELEPHONE OR ROOMS ARE AVAILABLE IN BALLARAT.

Twenty Three miles south of the access to Ballarat, is the town of **TRONA** which offers complete services, including as interesting historic museum. The Old Guest House Museum is located at 13193 Main Street, Trona, CA 93592. Phone (760) 372-4800.

Five miles south of Trona is the access road to **TRONA PINNACLES NATIONAL NATURAL LANDMARK**. The Trona Pinnacles are located seven miles south of Highway 178 off of a graded dirt road. If there have been recent rains it would be advisable to contact the local Bureau of Land Management office in Ridgecrest at (760) 375-7125 to see if the road is passable.

These large tufa formations were formed between 10,000 and 100,000 years ago when Searles Lake was some 640 feet deep. This area has been used as a backdrop in numerous films. **NOTE: THERE ARE NO FACILITIES HERE, NO RESTROOMS, AND NO WATER.**

Highway 395 may be accessed by continuing west on Highway 190 through Ridgecrest, 33 miles, or turning left, south, on Trona-Red Mountain Road 25 miles.

SECTION "D" - LAS VEGAS TO TONOPAH
208 Miles

Map Courtesy of Nevada Department Of Transportation

SECTION "D" LAS VEGAS TO TONOPAH
208 Miles
Includes side trips to: *"A"* Ash Meadows & Death Valley Junction & the Amargosa Opera House, *"B"* Rhyolite, Titus Canyon. (Both access roads into Death Valley National Park)

LAS VEGAS TO TONOPAH (HIGHWAY 95)
0 Mile 208
(The mileage to the left of the word "Miles" is from Las Vegas, to the right is from Tonopah)

This trip is made on Nevada Highway 95 which is partially divided and partially not, but it is paved and free of steep grades or mountainous twists and turns.

Heading northward from Las Vegas on Highway 95 it becomes increasingly evident how rapidly this entire area is growing. There is mile after mile of new housing developments. It is as almost as if Las Vegas has no ending.

Once the highway leaves "civilization" it heads up Las Vegas Valley with the Spring Mountains to the west and the 1,588,459-acre Desert National Wildlife Range to the east. The Desert Wildlife Range gives way to portions of Nellis Air Force Base and to the Nuclear Test Range as the road heads northward.

FLOYD LAMB STATE PARK
15 Mile 193
DETAILED INFORMATION ABOUT THIS PARK IS FOUND ON PAGE 8.

MOUNT CHARLESTON LOOP/SPRING MOUNTAIN RECREATION AREA
Mount Charleston, Deer Creek, Bristlecone Pine forest
A 36-Mile "Loop": Highways 157 West, 158 North, 156 East
21 Mile 187
Lodge, Hotel, Gas, Food & Camping

Located within an hour of Las Vegas, the Mount Charleston area offers attractions at virtually any time of the year. This mountainside area offers: 25 to 30 degree reductions in summer temperatures, numerous waterfalls in the spring, changes of colors in the fall and skiing and snow boarding in the winter.

Located at an altitude ranging from 8,000 to nearly 12,000 feet this mountainside is rich in the trees and vegetation missing from the valley floor below. There is camping available at 5 campground in most of the areas near the end of the "loop"

There are two hotels located on the mountain: Mount Charleston Lodge, (702) 872-5408 and Mount Charleston Hotel, (702) 872-5500.

At the top end of Highway 157 is the Mount Charleston Lodge: This "A" frame resort offers a large balcony overlooking Echo Peak and the surrounding mountains. Food is available either on the balcony or inside by the large fireplace.

One of the many views from the Mount Charleston Lodge balcony

There are many hiking trails through this area and a riding stable awaits horse renters. The hearty hiker can "assault" Mount Charleston, nearly 12,000 feet high.

In the Spring Mountain area of the Mount Charleston Loop is a grove of bristlecone pines. Among these ancient trees, which average 2500 years in age, is one REAL OLD tree. This tree is estimated to be 4,200 years old. Which tree is it?

The rangers won't tell. The rangers won't tell because if no one knows which tree is "Methuselah" it has a much better chance of not being abused by souvenir seekers. This grove is located along the North Loop Trail just below Mummy Mountain off of Highway 158 between Kyle and Lee Canyons. Additional information is available from the Kyle Canyon Ranger Station (702) 872-7098 or U.S. Forrest Service, Las Vegas, at (702) 873-8800

CORN CREEK FIELD STATION
DESERT NATIONAL WILDLIFE RANGE. (East side of the highway)
30 Mile 168
No services, small unstaffed visitor alcove with maps
NOTE: THIS IS LOCATED BETWEEN THE LEGS OF THE MOUNT CHARLESTON LOOP

On the east side of the highway this 4-mile gravel road leads to the Corn Creek Field Station and picnic area. There are numerous dirt roads in the area but are subject to closure as the animals are the prime concern in this area.

This 1,588,459-acre wildlife range was set up to primarily provide protection and the ability to observe and study the big horn sheep. Mule deer and other small mammals and birds are also studied.

Information: Refuge Manager, Desert National Wildlife Refuge, 1500 North Decatur Blvd., Las Vegas, Nevada 89108, (702) 646-3401

JUNCTION HIGHWAY 156
35 Mile 173
The northern end of the Mount Charleston Loop/Spring Mountain Recreation Area
(From page 79)
No Services

INDIAN SPRINGS
47 Mile 161
Food & Gas, motel, RV Park

Indian Springs offers a coffee shop, a few slot machines, a motel, RV Park and a gas station. This is also the site of Creech Air Force Base, formerly known as Indian Springs Air Force Auxiliary Air Field. Harrier jets have been spotted here.

Artesian springs in the area have been the cause of use of the area from earlier Native Americans, the railroad and today's population.

MERCURY
The Nevada Nuclear Test Site
65 Mile 143
No Services/NO ENTRY

"Camp Mercury" located 5 miles east of Highway 95 and it once had a population of 10,000. From 1951 through 1992 this 1,350 square mile site was the prime test center for nuclear fission by this country. Some 100 weapons were detonated above ground and an additional 828 were detonated below ground during this period of time.

During this period a complete city which included: a bowling alley, cafeteria and movie house had been provided for the workers and their families. Since the nuclear disarmament agreements while there are still personnel at Camp Mercury, the "city" is no longer in existence.

The 928 nuclear devices, which have been detonated at this site, have changed not only the shape of history, but also the shape of the earth. Areas such as Frenchman's Flat and Yucca Flat contain craters and holes and in some cases, massive amounts of radiation.

If you have the desire to tour The Nevada Test Site, see Page 5 of this book. **NOTE: Visitation is by APPOINTMENT ONLY.**

JUNCTION HIGHWAY 160
73 Mile 135

This is the "back way" into Pahrump, 17 miles, Mountain Springs 57 miles and Interstate 15, south of Las Vegas 76 miles. Also by taking Highway 372 (which becomes Highway 178 in California), there is access to Shoshone 51 miles, Death Valley 80 miles and Baker California 109 miles. A shorter route from Las Vegas to these areas is found on page 62.

ASH MEADOWS NATIONAL WILDLIFE REFUGE & DEVILS HOLE ACCESS; from this point will be find on Page 89

JUNCTION HIGHWAY 373, WEST (SIDE TRIP "A"- ACCESS TO DEATH VALLEY)
LATHROP WELLS/FORT AMARGOSA
90 Mile 118
Gas, Food, supplies, Lodging, Rest Area, RV park
Amargosa Valley 4 miles
Ash Meadows National Wildlife Refuge 14 miles. Page 88
Death Valley Junction 23 miles Amargosa Opera House Page 91
Death Valley National Park (Furnace Creek Center) 51 miles, Page 68

CARRARA (SITE)
Ruins East Side of Highway
112 Mile 96

Carrara today

The ruins on the hill to the east of the highway are all that is left of Carrara, a once flourishing mining town: a MARBLE mining town.

In 1907 a visitor to Beatty noticed an unusual formation on the hillside above the roadway. Upon investigation it was determined that the hills contained marble. The mining for marble did not begin until 1910-1911.

Quite a town sprung up at the site, complete with fountains and two parks.

The marble was mined in blocks which were four feet square and up to twelve feet in length and from as deep as 150 feet. The marble was to then be cabled down the hill to the railroad. Only one load was shipped when it was determined that the marble had been fractured beyond reasonable use by volcanic and earthquake activity in the area

The marble continued to be mined and was ground for use as cement into the 1940's.

BEATTY, NEVADA, Junction of Highway 374
119 Mile 89
All Services including a medical clinic
Rhyolite Ghost Town, Death Valley & Titus Canyon east on Highway 374 (SEE PAGE 89)
Beatty Chamber of Commerce, 119 Main St. P.O. Box 956, Beatty, NV 89003
(775) 553-2424 or (866) 736-3716 www.beattynevada.org

Much of Beatty is nestled in a green valley along a streambed, and can be likened to an oasis by the desert traveler. This "crossroads" town was founded around the turn of the century. Only recently, the largest mine in the area, The Bullfrog Mine, ceased operation. Like so many of the other mining towns in the area, Beatty has recently experienced a decrease in population.

Beatty is located at the crossroads of Highway 95 and Nevada State Route 374 (The Death Valley Highway) Beatty was founded as a supply town. At one time three different railroads intersected in Beatty. Partially because of her role as a supply center Beatty continued to thrive, as the mining towns around her "died."

Beatty contains a **Historical Society Museum**, at 417 West Main Street, (775) 553-2303, which is open daily. Starting in 1995 in a small cottage the museum is currently located in a historic church. This museum is one of the more complete museums insofar as exhibits from a local area are concerned. The museum was only recently expanded and offers the visitor an opportunity through numerous dioramas composed of authentic materials to experience the history and growth of the area.

SIDE TRIP "D-2" BEGINS AT THIS POINT (SEE PAGE 89)
Rhyolite Ghost Town, Titus Canyon alternate route, Death Valley National Park

JUNCTION HIGHWAY 267, SCOTTY'S JUNCTION
155 Mile 53
Gas & food.
Access to Scotty's Castle, Death Valley National Park 26 Miles

JUNCTION HIGHWAY 266 (Highway 395, NEXT SERVICES, Big Pine California 81 Miles)
170 Mile 38

Highway 266, an all-weather highway gives access from Nevada's Highway 95 to California's Highway 395. This highway also gives access to the Ancient Bristlecone Pine Forest, described in our *California's Highway 395 Windshield Adventures* . This highway crosses three mountain summits en route, check weather conditions in winter.

The ruins of several settlements are found along this route. One of the more interesting of these settlements is Palmetto, located 8 miles east of the California border. The name Palmetto was the result of the locals thinking that the Joshua Trees were related to palm trees. Between 1903 and 1906 Palmetto grew to a town that boasted a commercial district that was over ½ mile long.

The picture to the left shows one of the three passes along Highway 266 between Highways 95 and 395.

GOLDFIELD
(A GHOST TOWN THAT IS STILL ALIVE!)
182 Mile 26
Gas, Food, Lodging, supplies
Located on State Highway 95, 26 miles south of Tonopah and 182 miles north of Las Vegas
All Services

Once Goldfield was the largest city in Nevada. As it grew, it became a major trade center between the eastern and western portions of our growing country. Goldfield's history actually began with the exploration of the area just west of what is now Goldfield by two prospectors who had come south from Tonopah in 1902 in search of gold.

The historic Goldfield Hotel as she stands today

Soon other prospectors worked their way into the area and gold was being mined throughout the region. Late in May of 1903 the Combination lode was discovered and several weeks later a major strike was made there.

"Old west" tales have it that in 1903 this tent cabin town was named "Grandpa" by the miners in anticipation of this becoming the grand daddy of mining camps.

By 1904 the estimated population of what was now being called "Goldfield" was 8,000 and newspaper reports have $10,000.00 per day being mined there.

The ground continued to supply the riches and the town's growth continued. In 1905, the Tonopah & Goldfield Railroad arrived in town. There was a newspaper and extensive building going on now. By September of 1906 one mine was producing up to $40,000.00 per day from two shafts. Near the end of 1906 the population had passed 15,000 with some 150 buildings going up MONTHLY. Goldfield was a boomtown, a real "grandpa" of mining camps.

Soon the Las Vegas & Tonopah railroad came to Goldfield bringing in more and more miners and merchants. On Labor Day in 1906 a local promoter brought the world's lightweight boxing championship fight between Oscar "Battling" Nelson and Joe Gans to Goldfield. Eventually Goldfield was to become the home for five banks, three newspapers, several mining stock exchanges, five railroads and a population of 20,000 plus people.

In 1907 friction between the mine owners and the unions began to hamper development of the mining in the area. That series of conflicts, coupled with the financial reaction to the 1906 San Francisco earthquake, brought about the beginning of the end of Goldfield's golden era. Two of the town's three banks shut down.

In 1908 a slow recovery began and Goldfield became the county seat for Esmeralda (Spanish for emerald) County. In 1910 some 11 1/4 million dollars in bullion was produced here. However, soon the mines began to play themselves out and in 1913 a flash flood destroyed much of the town and some of the mining operations. In 1923 a fire destroyed some 54 square blocks of Goldfield.

There are numerous historically interesting buildings located in Goldfield. A home once owned by "Tex" Richard and the Santa Fe Saloon, built in 1905 are just several, others are found on the Goldfield map found on page 87.

Even though most of the people have left Goldfield, they left much of their history behind. In fact, today, there are numerous hotels in Las Vegas which can house more people than the total of all the citizens who reside in Esmeralda County

Beginning in 2,000 the County of Esmeralda began "Goldfield Days." The annual events have featured auctions of land parcels in and around Goldfield. In addition to the auctions there have been numerous other festivities. The result of these real estate auctions has been an influx of people into the area. In 2006, 26 parcels were sold out of 26 parcels offered. Contact the Esmeralda County Clerk and Treasurer for additional information: **Esmeralda County Clerk and Treasurer**, 233 Crook Street, Goldfield, NV 89013

A portion of the parade for the first annual Goldfield Days Festival

The skyline of Goldfield is dotted with many historical buildings including a beautiful stone courthouse, a rapidly deteriorating 3-story high school building and a 4 story luxurious hotel. The historic and beautiful hotel, the Goldfield Hotel, pictured, has not seen a paying guest since the 1940s, stands magnificently and almost fully restored awaiting a buyer.

This historic beauty, ever so close to complete restoration, stands vacant with the only inhabitants an occasional pigeon who wanders their way into the ambience of yesterday.

In the early 1990's restoration was begun on the Goldfield Hotel. The electrical and sprinkler systems for the bottom three floors have been replaced. All of the framing and sheet rock and most of the wooden wainscoting for the ground floor are complete. A stairway, to meet current fire codes, to the fourth floor has been completed. A new elevator shaft has been completed along with a new room designated as the kitchen. Even the heating and air conditioning are almost ready to go to work. But due to financial shortcomings on the part of the entity which began its restoration this magnificent structure sits empty with most of the materials required to complete the job inside. The grand old hotel sitting right on the state highway through Goldfield, still beckons to the passing traveler.

Several motion pictures have been filmed here in Goldfield. One which shows much of the town during car chases and shows the Goldfield Hotel, as a radio station, was "Vanishing Point."

Several other large historic buildings sit awaiting either assistance, or a slow death from age. At this time the citizens of Goldfield are attempting to save the Goldfield High School building which was in use from 1907 to 1953 and is rapidly decomposing

There is a mining equipment exhibit of at the library, located on the west side of the highway at the north end of town.

A brief shower wets an abandoned mine site, outside of Goldfield

A map showing the location of the attractions in Goldfield is shown on the following page.
    Goldfield Chamber of Commerce, 165 Creek Ave., Goldfield NV 89013, (775) 485-3560
    Goldfield Historical Society, P.O. Box 393, Goldfield, NV 89013

Leaving the town of Goldfield the Highway 95 makes a curve to the right. Several miles north of the main area of Goldfield there is a large cement structure to the right, east, side of the highway.

This structure is all that remains of a mill which once serviced the mines in the Goldfield area. The size of the structure gives some idea of the quantity of material which came from the mines in the earlier days.

SILVER PEAK TURN OFF
186 Mile 22
Silver Peak & Blair 25 miles
No services

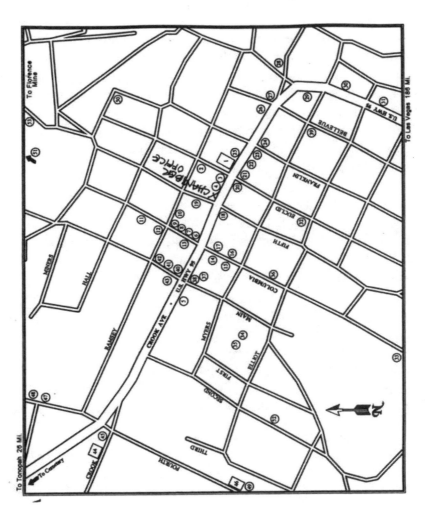

GOLDFIELD NEVADA

1. Esmeralda County Court House 1907
2. Goldfield High School 1907
3. Methodist Church 1912 / Goldfield Community Center
4. Rectory 1912 / Goldfield Chamber of Commerce
5. Mohawk Saloon site 1905 / Goldfield Candy Company
6. Kris Dairy Store 1923 / Roaring Camp
7. Montezuma Club site 1907
8. Curtis Ish Bldg. 1907
9. Nixon Wingfield Bldg. 1907
10. Telephone Office 1906
11. Cactus Club 1996
12. Elk's Hall 1923
13. Mozart Club 1934
14. Brown Parker Garage 1907 / Gloryhole
15. Lawyer's Office 1925
16. Florence Goldfield Mining Co. 1908
17. Goldfield Hotel 1908
18. Northern Cafe / Goldfield Brewery at the Northern 1950
19. Bartlett Mercantile 1905
20. Goldfield General Store
21. Goldfield Fire House 1908
22. Bottle House 1907
23. Tex Rickard 1907
24. Oasis Mini-Mart and Gas Station 1962
25. J. D. Carney Home 1908
26. J. A. Bayes Home 1908
27. John S. Cook Home 1906
28. Charles Sprague Home 1907
29. Ish Home 1907
30. Palm Front Saloon
31. Goldfield Motel
32. Thomas Lockhart Home 1908
33. Brewery Ruins 1905
34. Old Bordello 1907
35. First Jail 1903
36. M. L. Holt Home 1904
37. Dye Ormsby Bank Vault 1904
38. The Palace Saloon site 1904
39. Major William Anglus Station Home 1906
40. Northern Saloon site 1905
41. Men's Athletic Club site
42. Sideboard Saloon Arch 1907
43. The Hermitage Saloon site 1904
44. West Side School 1908 / Library
45. Historical Equipment Display
46. New Goldfield Post Office 1989
47. Gans / Nelson Prize Fight site 1906
48. Tonopah Goldfield Railroad site 1905
49. Last Outpost RV Park
50. White's RV and Trailer Park
51. Goldfield Days Ball Field
52. Goldfield Herb Mfg. 1905
53. Santa Fe Saloon 1905 / Motel

TONOPAH, NEVADA
"Queen of the Silver Camps"
MILE 189
Full Services including medical clinic
Tonopah Chamber of Commerce, P.O. Box 408, Tonopah, NV.89049, (775) 482-3558

Jim Butler was on a trip in central Nevada in May of 1900 He stopped near Sawtooth Pass. Next morning he looked up and one of his burros had run off. He picked up a rock to throw it but it was really heavy so he put it and a couple of others in his saddlebag. An assay of the rock showed a high silver content. Butler and his wife subsequently went back to the site in August and put up a whole bunch of claims.

Originally the town was called Butler in honor of its founder. The name Tonopah, Paiute for "Little Water", or "Small Spring" started catching on in 1902. The post office was still using Butler but when the town became the Nye County seat in 1904, it did so as Tonopah. Tonopah once had a population of over 10,000 people, but it's down from that at this time. Many of them came here because of the Tonopah Test Range that was home to the 117A Stealth fighter. Since the movement of the Stealth project from Nevada, it is hoped that mining, agriculture and other industries in the area will keep Tonopah alive.

The Central Nevada Museum, located west of Highway 95 at 1900 Logan Field Road, (775) 482-9676, is one of the most complete museums in Nevada. This museum is dedicated to the preservation and display of the history of all of central Nevada, including displays and information from Nye and Esmeralda Counties and numerous other communities in central Nevada.

The Tonopah Historical Mining Park (Fee area)
OPEN March 1st to October 31st, seven days a week, 9-5
November 1st to February 28th Friday through Sunday 10-4
520 McCulloch, P.O. Box 965, Tonopah, NV 89049 (775) 482-9274

The Tonopah Historical Mining Park was named the best rural attraction in Nevada from 2002 through 2006.

Desert Queen Mine- Photo courtesy of Tonopah Historic Mining Park

This ever-growing attraction is located on an over 100 acre site. The park is located on the site of the original claim of Belle and Jim Butler. Tours, both above and below ground, are available. This complete mine showcase features everything from hoist houses to the last remaining structure of the Tonopah and Goldfield Railroad. The exhibit halls include numerous exhibits. The facility shops also offer numerous displays. There is a gift shop. The annual Nevada State Mining Championships are held here

SIDE TRIP "D-1" HIGHWAY 373 WEST (FROM PAGE 82)

Ash Meadows 15 miles, Longstreet Inn 18 miles,
Death Valley Junction/Amargosa Opera House 23 miles, Furnace Creek, Death Valley 52 miles

ASH MEADOWS NATIONAL WILDLIFE REFUGE & DEVIL'S HOLE

MILE 15, No services
Ash Meadows NWR, HCR 70, Box 610Z, Amargosa Valley, NV 89020
(775) 372-5435, www.fws.gov/desertcomplex
Visitor Center open Monday thru Friday 8 am to 4:30 pm

So, what does 10,000-year old water look like? One look at the various springs of the Ash Meadows national Wildlife Refuge will tell you. The "fossil" water bubbling out of the many springs and seeps found in this oasis in the desert is what makes the Ash meadows Refuge a noticeably special place.

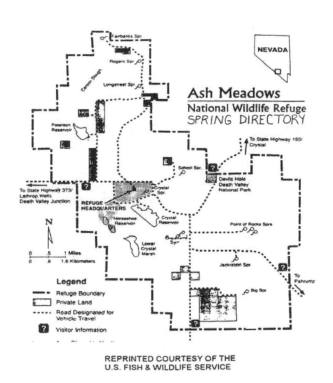

REPRINTED COURTESY OF THE
U.S. FISH & WILDLIFE SERVICE

Reprinted courtesy of the U.S. Fish & Wildlife Service

The water that feeds ash Meadows Refuge starts in its journey over 100 miles to the north, where it entered a vast underground aquifer system thousands of years ago. A geological fault below Ash Meadows acts as an "underground dam," blocking the flow of water in the subterranean aquifer and forcing it to the surface. Over 10,000 gallons-per-minutes flow from the many springs and seeps. These springs and the area surrounding them are home to at least 27 endemic species, including the Ash Meadows speckled dace, the Ash Meadows milk vetch, and the Ash Meadows naucorid found nowhere else on earth. Habitat destruction and the introduction of non-native species have caused seven of these native species to be listed as threatened and five as endangered.

The Ash Meadows National Wildlife Refuge was established in 1984 to protect threatened and endangered species and to conserve them in the wild. The area of Ash Meadows Refuge saw Southern Paiute and Timbisha Shoshone Indians, pioneers, ranchers, and farmers then it almost fell to the whims of developers before becoming a National Wildlife Refuge.

Because Ash Meadows Refuge is such a unique environment, it has been listed as a Wetland of International Importance with the Ramsar Convention, an international treaty among 136 countries.

Located inside the refuge boundaries, Devil's Hole National Park, part of the Death Valley National Park, is the home of the endangered Devil's Hole pupfish, which first gained recognition as the "most restricted vertebrate species in the world" and as an endangered species in the 1960's sites that should not be missed when visiting Ash Meadows Refuge include the Crystal Springs boardwalk Longstreet Spring and historic cabin, Peterson Reservoir and King's Pool at Point of Rocks, where a boardwalk will be put in place in 2007. Each of the springs stand between 80-90 degrees Fahrenheit and have clear water that gives the pools a bright blue hue.

The boardwalk at Crystal Springs Reservoir

Swimming or otherwise entering the springs is not allowed, as critical habitat could be damaged. All pets should be kept on a leash and are not allowed in the springs

Restrooms are available at the refuge office. Swimming is allowed at Crystal Reservoir, at your own risk. The public can access the refuge from sunrise to sunset. No overnight parking or camping is allowed. Please call the Refuge Manager for more information at: (775) 372-5435, seven days a week from 8:30 a.m. to 4 p.m.

GETTING THERE (*From Pahrump*) Take Bell Vista Road west about 22 miles. You will see the Ash Meadows National Wildlife Refuge sign on the north side of the road; turn on the dirt road after the sign. Pick up a visitor's map at the entrance sign for orientation. (*From Amargosa Valley, Lathrop Wells*) Head south on Highway 373, past the Imvite Facility. You will see the Ash Meadows National Wildlife Refuge sign on the west side of the road; turn east on the road after the sign. The pavement will give way to a dirt road once you come to our western boundary. Pick up a visitor's map at the entrance sign for orientation. (*From Death Valley Junction*) Head north on either Stateline Road, which becomes Bell Vista Road once you enter Nevada, or go north on Highway 127, which becomes Highway 373 once you enter Nevada. On Stateline Road, you will travel approximately 7 miles until you see the refuge sign on the south side of the road. Turn north on the dirt road after the sign. On Highway 127, head north to the Nevada border. You will continue on Highway 373 for approximately 3 more miles until you see the refuge sign on the west side of the road. Turn east on the paved road after the sign. The pavement will give way to a dirt road once you come to our western boundary. Pick up a visitor's map at the entrance sign for orientation.

LONGSTREET INN, CASINO, RV PARK & GOLF CLUB
Food (restaurant & mini-mart), lodging, RV Park, golf & casino. Gas, across the highway.
California/Nevada State Line - Hwy. 373
2 miles West of Ash Meadows 5 miles east of Death Valley Junction
HCR 70 Box 559, Amargosa Valley, Nevada 89020
(775) 372-1777 Fax (775) 372-1280 www.longstreetinn.com

Opened in 1966 and named for one of the true western characters, who had frequented the area, Longstreet is a true oasis in the desert.

With Death Valley's Funeral Mountains forming the western backdrop across the desert floor, the duck ponds, which are complete with fountains and waterfalls, and the greenery of the 9 hole executive golf course, make this a refreshing stopover when crossing the desert.

The new and modern full-service 60-room hotel offers several restaurants and a full casino. The RV guests are provided full hook-ups, including telephone and television and ample shower and laundry facilities.

The inn's namesake, Jack Longstreet, was one of those classic mysterious western characters like those depicted in the old dime novels; gunslinger, settler, miner, saloonkeeper, gambler, and a family man.

Little is known of Longstreet before he settled in the Ash Meadows area around 1880. He had a reputation as a hard drinker that carried a notched gun that had a taste for high-stakes poker.

DEATH VALLEY JUNCTION & THE AMARGOSA OPERA HOUSE
Hotel, Opera House (Performances 1st Saturday in October thru 1st Saturday in May @ 8:15 pm)
Reservations (Required,) & Information (775) 852-4441, www.amargosaoperahouse.com

P. O. Box 8, Death Valley Junction, CA 92328

Right out in the middle of, or maybe just a little to the right of, nowhere - one will find one of the most unusual and entertaining attractions to be found anywhere. How about an opera house, a beautifully hand decorated opera house complete with spectacular ballet, while wild horses and burrows wait for their dinner at the back door.

Just 29 miles east of Furnace Creek, Death Valley Junction has long been a focal point in the history of this part of the desert.

Death Valley Junction was born early in the summer of 1907 when the Tonopah & Tidewater Railroad opened a telegraph station at the site. The Tonopah & Tidewater was under construction at this time as it extended itself from Ludlow, California to Beatty, Nevada. At about the same time as the opening of the telegraph office in Death Valley Junction, a spur line was built from Death Valley Junction to borax mine located in Ryan, some seven miles to the southwest. The town began to grow not only because of the mine activity but it soon began to blossom as tourists arrived to take the stagecoach into Death Valley.

By 1915 Death Valley Junction had grown into quite a lively community complete with a school, boarding houses, additional stores and dormitories for the mill hands. In 1923-24-25 The Borax

Company erected the U-shape complex, which is now the Amargosa Opera House and Hotel. At the time of construction the building was intended for use as a company office & store, boarding house and hotel with a recreation hall at one end. Even when mining at Ryan ceased in 1927 this town continued to thrive. The tourists were continuing to arrive in Death Valley Junction especially after 1933 when Death Valley National Monument was created.

During the 1930's service and revenues from the Tonopah & Tidewater Railroad began to slow. In 1940 the railroad ceased operation. (Additional information on the Tonopah and Tidewater Railroad can be found in our first publication, "Windshield Adventuring Through the Mojave Desert." After the demise of the "T. & T." nearby farms and ranches kept the community alive.
In 1967 while on a dance tour of the west Marta and her husband had camped in Death Valley for several days. A flat tire on their camping trailer had sent them to Death Valley Junction.

Marta had visited Death Valley Junction during drizzle several years earlier. But on this trip, in the brilliant sunshine, she had discovered her destiny. It was obvious that the old community hall "Corkill Hall", at the northern end of the U-shaped hotel, had been abandoned for a long period of time and was in quite a bad state of repair.

Marta Becket realized that she had found "her place in the sun." Her thinking was that they would open the door and if people came, then it would be wonderful. If they didn't come she would still have her stage . . . her space . . . her empty canvas.

In addition to having found a place to exercise her talents, Marta has found another love here in the desert. Marta Becket has found love in the form of wild horses, which looks on as her children.

On February 10, 1968 the doors of the Amargosa Opera House opened for the first time and the curtain opened at promptly 8:15 to its first ballet in the desert. To this day the curtain always opens promptly at 8:15.

When one visits the Amargosa Opera House today Marta's talent at painting is quite evident, as she has decorated the entire interior of the theater, including the ceiling, with her paintings.
 The popularity of the ballet in Death Valley Junction's Amargosa Opera House has increased to the point where reservations are required, several months in advance is advisable. Marta Becket's Amargosa Opera House is now world-renowned. As the result of exposure through National Geographic Magazine, Life and Desert magazines and numerous other forms of exposure.

Shhh! Its 8:15 and the curtain is going up and the horses are out back just finishing their dinner!

Travel from Amargosa: #1. It is 29 miles via Highway 190 West, to Furnace Creek Center, Death Valley National Park, full services. #2. It is 30 miles south via Highway 127 to Shoshone, full services. NOTE: Page 65 offers several travel options from Shoshone.

END OF SIDE TRIP "D-1"
* * * * * * *

SIDE TRIP "D-2" (From Page 83)

Beatty to Rhyolite, Titus Canyon and Death Valley National Park via Highway 374
(Next services at Stovepipe Wells, 36 miles or Furnace Creek Center 41 miles.)

In the center of Beatty there is a "T" in the road. At the "T" Highway 95 North continues to the right and <u>Highway 374 goes to the left</u>. As a note; try not to miss stopping at the **Beatty Museum** (See Page 83) which is on highway 374 to your left just past the intersection with highway 95

After leaving Beatty Highway 374 goes up and then starts down a gentle hill. To the right are located the remnants of the *Bullfrog Mine* which was one of the major mines in the area. Just past the large tailings, 4 miles west of Beatty and to the right, is the signed entrance to Rhyolite.

RHYOLITE "THE QUEEN CITY" GHOST TOWN

Information center, Porta potties, phone.
(The large statues near the entrance to Rhyolite are not a part of Rhyolite)

The Cook Bank Building, "Downtown" Rhyolite

Located on a rolling plain, in what is referred to as the Bullfrog District stand the remains of what was once called the "Queen City of Nevada", Rhyolite. The term "Bullfrog" is derived from the color of gold bearing rock that the infamous Shorty Harris & E. L. Cross found here in 1904. Soon several camps sprung up in the area; the Bullfrog, Amargosa and an area referred to as Jumpertown. Soon a town site was laid out in the area, which became Rhyolite and was named after the mineral found in the area. At one point in history there were over 2000 claims in the 30-mile area covering the Bullfrog district. After it's beginning in 1904 Rhyolite literally exploded in population, this is while most mining towns, which sprang up in this era where little more than camps

After the initial influx of people into Rhyolite with their temporary shelters the growth of the town began heading towards more permanence in its structures. There was little wood in the immediate area so construction of rock and then cement buildings began.

As Rhyolite grew so did her services. A stock exchange and board of trade opened in Rhyolite. A total of three railroads came to town along with a hospital, two electric plants and a hospital. There was even an ice cream parlor! Rhyolite was born in 1905 and died in 1911, partially the result of investor panic created in part by the San Francisco earthquake of 1906. Today as one drives up the hill past the bottle house and past the remnants of the stone buildings towards the railroad station, yesterday might just appear.

The road continues past the three story remnants of the Cook Bank on the West Side of the street. One can almost see the 8,000 + citizens who resided here. The train station is off limits.

Some 30,000 visitors a year visit this ghost town. Recently, The Bureau of Land Management has opened an information center at the south end of town. The center has maps to help chart the location of the various buildings and attractions in Rhyolite.

The Rhyolite Train Station

The mining activity here at the Bullfrog Mine ended in late 1999 as the "load" has finally run out for Rhyolite & Bullfrog. The remnants of their operation are clearly visible as they the blanket hills behind the now vacant Rhyolite.

To reach Death Valley National Park you may stay on Highway 374 or if you have the proper vehicle, and it is not closed, choose to take the Titus Canyon Route.

TITUS CANYON (ALTERNATE "SCENIC" ROUTE INTO DEATH VALLEY)
THIS ROAD IS CLOSED IN SUMMER – No Services/No Camping
The turnoff to Titus Canyon from Highway 374 is 2 miles west of the turnoff to Rhyolite, 6 miles west of Beatty, Nevada. The road is signed, and one-way from this direction.

Petroglyphs along the roadside, traveling Titus Canyon

Titus Canyon Road is a picturesque and primitive 27-mile dirt road which is generally passable by vehicles with good ground clearance, no "low riders" here. Due to the nature of the road and possible effects the weather might have, it is advisable to check the current road conditions with the rangers in Death Valley (760) 786-2331. A portion of this road, if wet, is like trying to drive down hill on ice.

The route through Titus Canyon is one way and is entered from the east from Highway 374. Once the road enters the Grapevine Mountains it begins winding its way through switchbacks and features steep grades as it winds its way not to just one but two summits.

The highest of these summits, 5250 feet, is some 1500 feet above the Amargosa Desert from which it rises. This summit is 12 miles from the beginning of our road. This summit offers spectacular views in both directions, either from the road or after a short walk up from the turnoff located at the summit.

Three miles down the hill from the summit an interesting piece of history and greed is found. Here stand several metal buildings and a sign marking the location of Leadville. Leadville, conceived as a fraud, lasted from 1926 to 1927. A promoter duped the investors in Leadville by having "salted" the area to make it appear to be rich in ore.

Deep in Titus Canyon

Soon a road was built into the canyon at great expense and the town-site subdivided as stock was sold to the eager investors. Soon the California State Corporation Commission was investigating Charles Julian, the promoter who had perpetrated the Leadville fraud. Julian fled to Oklahoma where he was charged with mail fraud and subsequently, so the story goes, fled to Shanghai and died a year later at the age of 40.

Continuing another 2 miles down the hill from Leadville brings the traveler to Klare Springs. Klare Springs has been a source of water for men and animals for centuries. Petroglyphs mark the presence of the historic Native Americans who once frequented the area, while footprints and sightings verify the current use of the natural springs by big horn sheep and other animals.

Continuing into the canyon itself you enter into an area of primitive anticline where folds in the earth that have turned the rock layers upside down. The canyon itself is some 5 miles in length and it becomes narrower and narrower as you travel westward.

From the junction of Titus Canyon Road and Highway 190 it is 18 miles north to the Grapevine Ranger Station and 14 miles south to the junction of Highway 374.

END OF SIDE TRIP "D-2"

SECTION "E" SOUTHWESTERN UTAH

MILEAGE SHOWN IS FROM MESQUITE, NEVADA

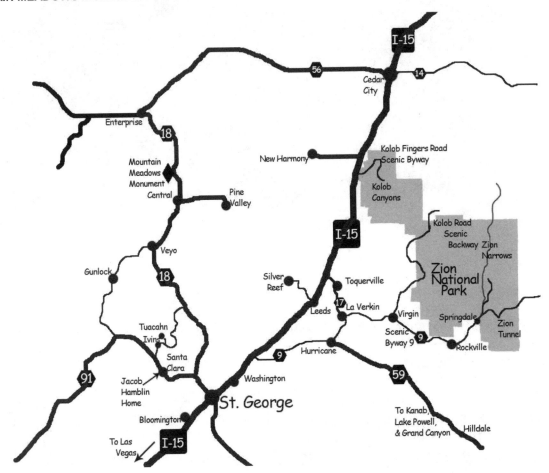

Map of southwestern Washington County, Utah, showing the attractions found in this section

MESQUITE, NEVADA, STARTING POINT (FROM PAGE 34)
HIGHWAY I-15 NORTH

Leaving Mesquite, Nevada, I-15 enters the state of Arizona. Soon the highway enters the **Virgin River Gorge Recreational Area**, which is both scenic and spectacular, lasting most of the way across this 18-mile portion of the northwest corner of Arizona.

There are numerous pullouts as the highway travels through the River Gorge Recreation Area. About mid-way through the canyon, at Exit 18 (Cedar Pockets Interchange) there is access into the recreation area. The main recreation area, including the year-round campground, is located south of the highway. There is access to the Virgin River from the upper campground.

The area is home to Bighorn Sheep and the numerous cliff faces are also popular with two legged rock climbers!

The northeastern end of the Virgin River Gorge Recreational Area is near the border of the state of Utah's Washington County.

UTAH'S WASHINGTON COUNTY

Utah's Washington County is home to many attractions. Two of the most historic and unusual are located on opposite sides of Interstate 15. To the east of Interstate 15 as it cuts northward from the glitz and glimmer of Las Vegas stands the famous and beautiful Zion National Park, **PAGE**. This place of historic beauty is an exact opposite of what lies some 30 miles to the west of the highway in a valley known as Mountain Meadows, **PAGE**.

ST GEORGE, UTAH, THE COTTON MISSION
Mile 26 from Mesquite (From Las Vegas to St. George 116 miles)
Full services including hospital

While there was an earlier settlement located just north of St. George at Washington, in 1861 Brigham Young, the Mormon leader at the time, directed some of his followers to move southward into the area which is now St. George. The purpose of this settlement was for growing cotton and cultivating silk worms. The climate in this area was much milder, and more conducive to cotton farming than found as a result of the severe winters found in the capital at Salt Lake City.

Today, St. George is a modern thriving city which maintains touch with its history through numerous historical locations and museums.

During the Mormon movement westward, scurvy was one of the dangers and a great number of the Mormon travelers perished as the result of it.

The town of St. George was named after a fellow whom had eaten the peelings off of his potatoes so that his family could eat the meat of the potatoes. This was done with the thought that he wanted his family to have the best part of the potatoes while he ate what was considered the worst part. His family died of scurvy during the trip west and he did not. At the time he was not aware that this was the result of the vitamin C in the peelings. Once he became aware of the value of the vitamin C in the peelings, this fellow went far and wide and preached "eat the peelings." This among other things caused Brigham Young to look upon him as a saint and named the town after him.

The city of St. George contains many interesting and historic sites, just a few of which are mentioned here.

McQUARRIE MEMORIAL/DAUGHTERS OF UTAH'S PIONEERS MUSEUM
145 North 200 East, St. George 84770
(435) 628-7274
M-S 10:00 – 5:00 Closed Holidays

Dedicated in June of 1938 this museum contains two complete floors of memorabilia and history. In 1985 a major addition was made to the museum.

The museum was originally funded by a donation of $17,500 to "house the relics of the Dixie Pioneers, the parents and grandparents who colonized the Dixie Cotton Mission."

Within the building is one of the most extensive exhibitions of what life was like at the time the area of St George was founded. There are numerous photos and paintings in addition to the regular exhibits.

BRIGHAM YOUNG'S WINTER HOME
89 West 100 North St. George UT, 84774
(435) 673-2517
Tours 9:00 – Dusk

Construction of this "winter home" for the leader of the L D S church (who was also the governor of the state of Utah) was begun in 1869 and completed in 1871. The front addition was completed in 1873.

The interior and exterior of the house retains the furnishings and other items from the time of its original usage.

Brigham Young used this home as his "winter retreat" from the harsh winters in the capital at Salt Lake City.

JACOB HAMBLIN HOME
3300 Block of Santa Clara Street, Santa Clara Utah
(From St. George; North on Bluff Street, West on Sunset Blvd. which becomes Santa Clara Street)

Jacob Hamblin was placed into the Cowboy Hall of Fame as the result of having ridden more miles on horseback than any other man who traveled the west. Much of Hamblin's riding was done in the pursuit of working towards peaceful relations with the Native Americans.

Born in Ohio in 1819 Hamblin soon moved to Wisconsin where he helped his father open new land for agriculture.

Married at the age of twenty in 1839, Hamblin decided to come west with the Mormon movement to Utah in 1850.

Soon after his arrival in the Salt Lake City area, Hamblin became convinced that the conflicts with the Native Americans could be replaced with honest negotiation. In 1854 Brigham Young appointed Jacob Hamblin as missionary to the Piute Indians in Southern Utah. It was through Hamblin's ledgers as he rode through the west on the mission of establishing peace with the Indians that the tremendous number of horseback miles ridden was determined.

The family moved into the area which is now known as Santa Clara and erected a rock fort in the creek bed below the site of the present house. In 1862 a flood swept through the area which destroyed the fort and caused the eventual death of one of Jacob's wives. (There are two chairs in the upstairs of the Hamblin house which are the only remnants of the original rock fort.)

In 1862 the existing Hamblin home was constructed on the side of the hill where it overlooks the valley in which the flood destroyed the original home. This home was constructed of local sandstone and Ponderosa timbers from the Pine Valley area.

The house stands today as it would as if it was being lived in over a hundred years ago when it was built. In addition to periodic furnishings the Hamblin House contains several items of historic interest including a copy of the famous Fort Defiance Navajo Indian treaty which came about primarily as a result of Hamblin's efforts.

Jacob Hamblin spent little time at his home with his wives and at times more than a dozen children. Jacob ranged throughout the west bringing peace with various Indian nations. Hamblin worked with the Navajo, Utes, Hopi and Moqui tribes among others.

In 1869 Hamblin sold this home and moved to the Kanab fort.

Hamblin made numerous trips into Arizona and is reported to be the first white man to ride entirely around the Grand Canyon.

Jacob continued his work as an explorer, pioneer and peacemaker throughout the remainder of his life. It has been suggested that had Jacob Hamblin been at home on September 11, 1857, the massacre at Mountain Meadows could have been averted.

Jacob Hamblin died at his home in Pleasanton, New Mexico in 1886.

ZION NATIONAL PARK, SOUTH (MAIN) ENTRANCE
Zion National Park, Springdale, Utah 84767 (435) 7723256
Zion Lodge (888) 297-2757
Mesquite, Nevada (Page 34) 69 miles.
From St. George it is 10 miles north to Highway 9, then East 34 miles to Zion Canyon
Visitor Center

FREE TOUR BUS OPERATION: Since April 2000 private vehicle traffic has been reduced within narrow Zion Canyon. Parking of private vehicles within the park has been reduced by having free parking within the town of Springdale. Look for the "Shuttle Parking" signs in town. The tour bus rides are free with the buses stopping at key points throughout Zion Canyon. The free shuttles generally run every 8 minutes, except in winter when parking is not a problem within the canyon.

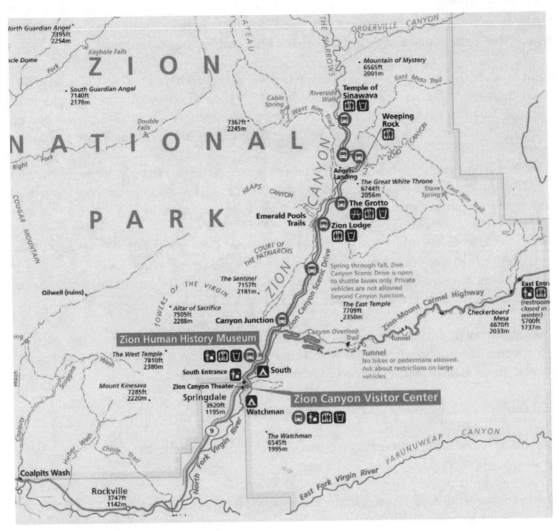

This map, courtesy of the National Park Service, shows the main features of the Zion Canyon area

The name "Zion" was initially given to the canyon by the Mormons in the 1860's as they considered it a place of safety and refuge.

In order to fully appreciate the features of Zion National Park, it is strongly recommended that the Zion Canyon Visitor Center be visited prior to entrance to the park

The park offers attractions for virtually all types of visitors. Many of the trails are "handicapped friendly." There are extreme hiking climbing opportunities in addition to paved pathways. At several of the attractions pathways are offered for people with different physical capabilities.

We have outlined here some of the more popular attractions in the main section of the park.

WEEPING ROCK This walk of 0.6-mile in each direction takes the traveler on a paved path across a stream and through the woods up to an unusual phenomenon, unusual in places other than the Zion area. The different textures of the rocks in the area become evident as the water from hundreds of feet above the canyon seeps through the more porous rock formations and then travel vertically through the rock bordering the canyon to where the water actually seeps through the sides of the canyon wall.

In many areas, such as Weeping Rock, the rock below the area, which is carrying the water out of the rock, is over the centuries eaten away by the water. The effect is that the water comes out of the rock and drops over the eroded area just like an extended waterfall. The walk up and down, is not that long or that strenuous.

THE RIVERSIDE WALK This walk is approximate 1 mile each way as it travels along the eastern bank of the Virgin River at the farthest end of the main portion of Zion Canyon. The paved walk gives the visitor access to not only the river in various stages but is also access to the "Narrows." The Narrows is located beyond the initial pathway and is a narrow canyon which was formed by the river as it ground its way, over the ages, through the stonewalls which supported it. Access above the end of the one-mile trail is gained by hiking the riverbed itself, which can be hazardous.

The author at the end of Riverside Walk/entrance to the Narrows

Any trips taken past the paved walk should be cleared through the NPS Ranger to ascertain the water level of the river, due to the danger of being caught in a flash flood in the narrow canyon.

EMERALD POOLS offers the hiker three variations of difficulty in reaching the same general area. The middle and upper Emerald Pool Trails are longer and more strenuous. The most popular for the "amateur" hiker is the Lower Trail, which takes the hiker along an improved trail for 0.6, miles in each direction, to a huge overhang with waterfalls along it. The trip up the canyon to the falls is spectacular in itself and the falls are a bonus.

Zion National Park offers more than just spectacular scenery to her visitors. Try a meal in the lodge followed by a warming fire in the fireplace in your cabin while deer are grazing on the lawn out front.

KOLOB CANYON, ZION NATIONAL PARK, NORTHWEST SECTION
Access is from I-15 Exit 40, 26 miles north of St. George & 17 miles south of Cedar City
Fee Area

This 10.6-miles round-trip drive is surely one of the most spectacular in the world.

Along the roadway into Kolob Canyon, western section of Zion National Park

The *Kolob Canyons Road Guide*, available at the Kolob Canyon Visitor Center office at the beginning of the drive offers a detailed guide to this trip over the hills and into one of the most spectacular canyons anywhere. The road climbs some 1100 feet but is paved and passable by any vehicle capable of making the climb. There are numerous pull-outs and trailheads along the drive.

CEDAR CITY
Iron County Tourism & Convention Bureau (800) 354-4849 & (435) 586-5142
581 North Main Street, Cedar City UT, 84720
Full services

This city booms during the tourist seasons. Summer sees Shakespearian Festivals and numerous other events. Off-season it is a quiet but beautifully located city. Cedar City is located at the base of the mountains which house the Cedar Breaks. In winter the red cliffs are highlighted with snow which also adorns the mountains further east.

VISITORS CENTER & DAUGHTERS OF UTAH PIONEERS MUSEUM
585 North Main Street, Cedar City UT 84720 (435) 586-4484

Across the parking lot to the south of the Mission State Park is the combination Visitor's Center and Daughters of Utah Pioneers Museum. The Visitor's Center offers maps and complete information on the numerous attractions in the area. This small museum is filled with items which were either brought westward prior to the railroad or which were made during that same period. It is our understanding that this unique museum is manned by daughters and granddaughters of the pioneers which certainly adds to the interest and knowledge available.

IRON MISSION STATE PARK
635 North Main Street, Cedar City Utah 84720-2127
(435) 586-9290
Fee Area

Cedar City is the site of the Iron Mission State Park. This unique park offers the visitor a look at much of what made up Utah in the 1800s and the early 1900s. Inside this building are found static displays, memorabilia, and a large collection of horse drawn and other vehicles. Out back are several log cabins, including the oldest structure still standing in the State of Utah.

MOUNTAIN MEADOWS MEMORIAL SITE
30 Miles north of St. George on Highway 18.
From Cedar City; 35 miles west on Highway 56 to Highway 18, 20 miles south

Getting to Mountain Meadows is a 45 to 60 minute drive from St. George Utah via Utah Highway #18, Bluff Street. Highway 18 intersects I-15 at the southern end of St. George and is a two lane paved road.

Mountain Meadows offers a pastoral beauty of a different nature. The green fields and rolling hills give no indication to the horror which occurred here in the mid-1850s. Yes, several monuments mark the area but unless one was to read the inscriptions on the monuments there would be no guessing of the real meaning of Mountain Meadows.

In 1857 Mountain Meadows was the site of the deaths of American citizens at the hands of other American citizens which was exceeded only by the bombing of the Oklahoma City Federal Building in 1995.

It was 1857 and the state of Utah and the government of the United States of America were at a point which was close to war. The Mormons had pulled most of the missionaries out of the western portion of the country and had them return to Salt Lake City. Even the Mormon Mission at Las Vegas was closed.

The United States Mail was being stopped at the Utah border and the United State Army was sending troops towards the Utah border. At this time Brigham Young sent emissaries into what is now eastern Nevada to seek out places to which the Mormons could be evacuated in the event of attack by the federal troops.

Into this arena of hostile feelings came the Baker/Fancher wagon train from Arkansas. The wagon train was traveling down the Spanish Trail headed for California. Since shortly after their arrival in Utah the Mormon settlers had started trading their produce for manufactured items being carried on the wagon trains traveling through Utah. Not so during this period in time.

Orders had come from Salt Lake City that no aid, assistance or trading was to be done with the "outsiders." Not only were there hostile feelings between the Mormons in the area towards non-Mormons, this particular group brought even more animosity with it. This wagon train had been in part originated in the same area of Illinois in which Joseph Smith, the founder of the Mormon Church, had been attacked and killed by a mob. It is unclear as to whether or not any of the members of this wagon train had actually participated in the death of Joseph Smith or not. It is reported, however, that there was taunting by members of the Illinois portion of train towards some of the Mormons in the area. When the wagon train reached Salt Lake City, it is reported that the Baker/Fancher portion of the train separated from the Illinois portion.

On September 7, 1857, shortly after the wagon train's arrival at Mountain Meadows, the Baker/Fancher came under siege by a group of Paiute Indians and local Mormon settlers dressed as Indians. The siege lasted for five days and kept the members of the train from reaching the nearby water. Some 15 of the wagon train members were killed and a score wounded during this five day period.

On the fifth day of the siege a group of Mormon militia from Cedar City, 35 miles to the northeast, arrived at the meadows. John D. Lee, a Mormon Bishop and leader of the militia group, approached the besieged wagon train under a flag of truce. Lee convinced the survivors of the wagon train that if they would leave their wagons and other goods for the Paiute and leave with him and his militia that the Indians would allow them to leave safely as the Mormon militia's prisoners.

After a short period of deliberation the survivors, who were desperate, agreed to Lee's terms. The wagon train party's weapons were loaded into one wagon and the younger children were loaded into other wagons

The wagons loaded with the weapons and small children led the way out of the encampment. Following the wagons on foot, came the older children and the women. Behind the women came the men in a single file line, flanked by the Mormon militia.

The upper memorial lists the names of the victims

About a mile northeast of the remaining wagons, which were now being looted by the Indians, Bishop Lee stood up in his stirrups and exclaimed "Do your duty." On that command, the Mormon militia shot all of the male prisoners. At about the same time Mormons disguised as Indians, and some of the actual Indians began the slaughter of the women and the children shooting, clubbing and axing them to death.

The massacre cost the lives of some 120 people. There were some children who survived, most of which were returned to Arkansas sometime after the massacre.

On March 23, 1877 after several trials, John Doyle Lee was executed at this site. Lee was the only person convicted of the 1857 massacre.

The site itself is divided into two sections. The Mormon Monument is located in the meadow itself and is accessed by an unmarked dirt road just a few feet from the highway to the left of the paved monument access road. The dirt road to the monument in the valley is approximately ½ mile long and accessible by any vehicle.

The L.D.S. Church memorial marks the mass gravesite

The lower monument, built by the L D S church is marked by a large American Flag, is reached via a short walk from a parking area.

This monument marks the site of the graves of some of the people who were killed during the massacre and the five-day siege. The massacre site is approximately a mile north of this monument and can be spotted through a viewing tube, located at the site of the upper monument, which is located atop the bluff to the north and east of this location.

Working farms and ranches surrounds this entire area. There is nothing left of the massacre to be found here and it makes no sense to traipse through some farmer's field searching for a souvenir, please refrain from crossing fences or closed gates.

The upper monument is located off the signed, paved road about ¼ mile from the highway. There is a large paved parking area and the monument is located a short walk west of the parking lot via a paved path The upper monument is located on a bluff overlooking Mountain Meadows. This area contains; a cement monument which lists the names of the victims of the massacre, several plaques and viewing tubes allowing the visitor to spot the location of the initial attack and the location of the actual massacre. There are benches at the site and along the path leading up to the monument site.

Upon leaving the memorial site, traveling north on Highway 18 approximately 20 miles to Highway 56 then east 35 miles will take the traveler into Cedar City

* * * * * * * *

Author's note: So ends this "Windshield Adventuring Book." We hope that you have enjoyed it!

We have left you here in southern Utah, at the gateway to many of the more spectacular spots in the entire world. Included in this circle, in addition to Zion National Park, are other attractions in Utah, in Arizona, western Colorado and in northern New Mexico.

Perhaps, just perhaps, you can join us, in another book as we explore "The Grand Circle."

Russell & Kathlynn Spencer, the Windshield Adventurers.